GCSE
WJEC German

REVISION GUIDE
FOR THE NEW GCSE (2018 ONWARDS)

Chris Whittaker and
Bethan McHugh

Crown House Publishing
www.crownhouse.co.uk

First published by

Crown House Publishing Ltd

Crown Buildings, Bancyfelin, Carmarthen, Wales, SA33 5ND, UK

www.crownhouse.co.uk

and

Crown House Publishing Company LLC

PO Box 2223

Williston, VT 05495, USA

www.crownhousepublishing.com

Cover image © Alfonso de Tomás, © dikobrazik, © robodread – Fotolia.com.
Icons, pages 4–5, 9, 11, 13, 15, 17, 25, 41, 106–133, © schinsilord – Fotolia.
Page 7, © LuckyImages – Fotolia: Pages 18–19, © JB Fontana – Fotolia: Page 21, © Milkos – Fotolia: Page 23, © micromonkey – Fotolia: Page 27, © talitha – Fotolia: Pages 28–29, © Brian Jackson – Fotolia: Page 31, © belekekin – Fotolia: Page 32, © BillionPhotos.com – Fotolia: Page 33 (t), © freshidea – Fotolia: Page 33 (b), Lsantilli– Fotolia: Page 34, © WavebreakMediaMicro – Fotolia: Page 36, © corund – Fotolia: Page 37, © Focus Pocus LTD – Fotolia: Pages 38–39, © Svenni – Fotolia: Page 42, © Dylan Randell: Page 43 (t), © Aliaksei Lasevich – Fotolia: Page 43 (b), © eivaisla – Fotolia: Page 45, © Thaut Images – Fotolia: Page 46, © Farina3000 – Fotolia: Page 47, © JackF – Fotolia: Pages 48–49, © andyastbury – Fotolia: Page 53 (t), © silver-john – Fotolia: Page 53 (b), © saknarong – Fotolia: Page 55, © JFL Photography – Fotolia: Page 56, © lucadp – Fotolia: Page 57, © connel_design – Fotolia: Pages 58–59, © Black Spring – Fotolia: Page 62, © berc – Fotolia: Page 63, © Zerophoto – Fotolia: Page 65, © jarek106 – Fotolia: Page 67, © zhu difeng – Fotolia: Pages 68–69, © peshkov – Fotolia: Page 72, © korionov – Fotolia: Page 73, © icsnaps – Fotolia: Page 75, © sanchos303 – Fotolia: Page 76, © niroworld – Fotolia: Page 77, © Monkey Business – Fotolia: Pages 78–79, © sebra – Fotolia: Page 81, © Vladimir Melnikov – Fotolia: Page 82, © Monkey Business – Fotolia: Page 83, © famveldman – Fotolia: Page 85, © Antonio Gravante – Fotolia: Page 87, © Christian Schwier – Fotolia: Pages 88–89, © mikola249 – Fotolia: Page 91 (t) © Tamara Kulikova – Fotolia: Page 91 (b), © zhu difeng – Fotolia: Page 93, © pathdoc – Fotolia: Page 95, © djile – Fotolia: Page 97, © goodluz – Fotolia: Page 99, © connel_design – Fotolia: Page 101 (t), © vege – Fotolia: Page 101 (b), © Syda Productions – Fotolia: Page 104, © Olivier Le Moal – Fotolia: Page 105, © javiindy – Fotolia.

British Library of Cataloguing-in-Publication Data

A catalogue entry for this book is available from the British Library.

Print ISBN 978-178583275-8

Printed and bound in the UK by Pureprint Group, Uckfield, East Sussex

CONTENTS

INTRODUCING WJEC GCSE GERMAN

Your WJEC German GCSE is split into three main themes:

- IDENTITY AND CULTURE
- WALES AND THE WORLD – AREAS OF INTEREST
- CURRENT AND FUTURE STUDY AND EMPLOYMENT

Your four German exams (SPEAKING, LISTENING, READING and WRITING) will cover these three themes equally. Each exam is worth 25% of your final grade. You are not allowed to use a dictionary in any exam.

Now for the confusing bit! Each of these three themes has sub-themes which are divided into sections. These sections are all of equal importance – so don't spend all of your time concentrating on your favourites! Make sure you revise all the topics equally.

IDENTITY AND CULTURE	WALES AND THE WORLD – AREAS OF INTEREST	CURRENT AND FUTURE STUDY AND EMPLOYMENT
YOUTH CULTURE • Self and relationships • Technology and social media	**HOME AND LOCALITY** • Local areas of interest • Travel and transport	**CURRENT STUDY** • School/college life • School/college studies
LIFESTYLE • Health and fitness • Entertainment and leisure	**THE WIDER WORLD** • Local and regional features and characteristics of Germany and German-speaking countries • Holidays and tourism	**ENTERPRISE, EMPLOYABILITY AND FUTURE PLANS** • Employment • Skills and personal qualities • Post-16 study • Career plans
CUSTOMS AND TRADITIONS • Food and drink • Festivals and celebrations	**GLOBAL SUSTAINABILITY** • Environment • Social issues	

This revision guide covers all of the themes and sub-themes, as well as giving tips and advice on how to prepare for each exam with plenty of exam-style questions and grammar practice to help you. Viel Glück!

Note: English will be referred to throughout this revision guide as the native language in which to provide answers and to translate into/from German. If, however, you are studying WJEC GCSE German through the medium of Welsh, then please substitute 'Welsh' for 'English' accordingly.

SPEAKING EXAM

The first exam you will do is the speaking one. This is usually quite a bit earlier than the other three exams. The whole exam will last about 20 minutes, including your preparation time. This is what will happen:

1. You will go to a preparation room with an invigilator and you will be given a booklet. This booklet contains your role play, photo card and choices for the conversation. You will have 12 minutes to prepare for the exam and make notes. You can't write full sentences or a script but you should have time to think about what you are going to say and note some useful keywords and phrases.

2. Once your preparation time is up, you will go into the exam room with your teacher. You will take your notes with you. Once the teacher has recorded your name, candidate number, etc. the exam will begin. You will complete the role play, then the photo card and finally the conversation. The recording will not be stopped between each section.

ROLE PLAY

Your role play will look something like this:

Setting: Your German friend has come to visit and you are talking about health. Your teacher will play the part of your German friend.

Your teacher will speak first.

- Say what sport you do.
- Give an opinion on fast food.
- Answer the question.
- Ask your friend what he/she does to stay healthy.
- Say what you ate yesterday.

There will be a sentence at the start in English which is the 'setting' and explains the theme of the role play. Don't worry too much about this. The important bit here is the theme – health, in this example – and the part, which tells you who will speak first (usually but not always your teacher).

There are **five** bullet points in every role play. Make sure you answer in a complete sentence.

When you see **Answer the question** you will have to respond to a question you have not prepared for. In your preparation time try to think of the sort of thing which you may be asked.

You will also have to **ask** a question. This could be quite a simple question – e.g. Rauchst du?

At Foundation level one of the prompts will be in a different tense (usually the past). Watch out for clues like yesterday, last year and last weekend. At Higher level there will be two prompts in a different tense. Look out for clues prompting you to use the future or conditional – e.g. tomorrow, next week, in the future.

Unlike with other parts of the speaking exam, you won't get any extra marks for adding in further details, opinions, etc. In the role play you only have to give the information asked for in the bullet points and nothing more.

You may have to give an opinion or point of view. It doesn't matter whether you really think this or not as long as you say something.

Try to answer in a complete sentence using an appropriate verb – e.g. Fast Food ist lecker not just lecker.

PHOTO CARD

You will have your photo and **two** questions in advance, so there is no excuse for not having full, extended answers ready. Your teacher doesn't want you to read a script, but you should have a good idea of what to say. Your card will look something like this:

- Beschreibe das Foto./Was passiert auf diesem Foto?
- Feierst du lieber mit Freunden oder Familie? Warum?

The first question on the photo card will always ask you to describe the photo. There is no fixed amount you have to say but you should be aiming for at least **three** or **four** details for maximum marks – e.g. Who is in the photo? What are they doing? Where are they? Why are they there? What else is in the photo? What do you think about the photo?

The second question will usually ask for an opinion. Try to elaborate as much as you can. Make sure you justify and explain your opinions and give as much information as possible.

UNSEEN QUESTIONS

Your teacher will then ask you **two** unseen questions. In the first unseen question you will usually have to comment on an opinion – e.g.:

- Geburtstagspartys sind sehr teuer. Was sagst du dazu? Birthday parties are very expensive. What do you think?

The last question will usually need to be answered in a different tense – e.g.:

- Was hast du an deinem letzten Geburtstag gemacht? What did you do for your last birthday?
- Was wäre deine Traumparty? What would your dream party be like?

In your preparation time try to think of some of the things you might be asked in the unseen questions. Listen carefully to what the teacher says and don't guess – if you don't understand, ask them to repeat the question. You won't lose any marks and this will buy you extra thinking time! You don't have to agree with the opinion given by the teacher.

Here are some useful phrases and questions:

Deiner Meinung nach	In your opinion
Beschreibe	Describe
Warum sagst du das?	Why do you say that?
Warum (nicht)?	Why (not)?
Was denkst du?	What do you think?
Magst du lieber ...?	Do you prefer ...?
Was passiert ...?	What is happening ...?
Was sind die positiven/negativen Aspekte?	What are the positive/negative aspects?
Was sind die Vorteile/Nachteile?	What are the advantages/disadvantages?

CONVERSATION

The conversation lasts for 3–5 minutes (Foundation) and 5–7 minutes (Higher). This is split equally between two parts.

- Part 1 – You will be given a choice of sub-themes. You will start this part of the conversation by saying what you have chosen to talk about.
- Part 2 – This will be on a different theme and you will have a choice of sub-themes.

The conversation is your chance to show off the full extent of your knowledge of the language. What you say doesn't have to be factually correct as long as your German makes sense! You need to make sure that you are able to give some answers in the past, present and future tenses to access the highest marks. Try to give additional detail, opinions and justifications wherever possible and include some complex phrases.

If you get stuck ...?

- If you don't understand a question, ask your teacher to repeat it.
- Don't worry if you can't remember a particular word, say something else instead.
- If you make a mistake, it's okay to correct yourself.

LISTENING EXAM

In the listening exam you can expect to hear different types of spoken language which may include monologues, conversations, discussions, interviews, announcements, adverts and messages.

- Before the exam starts, you will have 5 minutes reading time. Don't waste this time filling in your name and candidate number! Use the time to read the questions carefully and make sure you know what you have to do, etc. Make a note of any keywords and phrases which may be useful.
- Read the questions and make sure you are giving the required information – e.g. what, why, when, etc. Pay attention to negatives. The question 'Which hobby does she like?' requires a very different answer to 'Which hobby does she **not** like?'
- The paper will usually start with the easier questions and get harder throughout.
- You will hear each extract twice.
- There are **nine** questions but they are not all worth the same amount of marks. There are some 4, 5 and 6 mark questions so make sure you pay attention to this!
- Check carefully how many marks are available for the question. If you are asked to tick four boxes, make sure you don't tick more than four. You will lose marks if you do.
- Read the question carefully and listen to the recording for any keywords related to the question. Check the question again to make sure you are clear exactly what is being asked. Listen to the recording for a second time. Finalise your answer.
- There will be **two** questions in German on your paper. You won't know where they will be until you see your paper and they might not be next to each other. They will probably ask for an answer in the form of a tick or a letter, etc. but you might have to write something in German. If you answer in English you won't get the mark, even if it's right. Always answer in the same language as the question.
- Don't leave any answers blank. Have an educated guess!

READING EXAM

In the reading exam you can expect to see a range of texts of different lengths, written in formal and informal styles and for a variety of audiences – e.g. magazine articles, information leaflets, adverts, literary texts, etc.

- Like the listening exam, the reading paper will usually start with the easier questions and gradually get harder – but the translation into English will always be the last question.
- There will be **two** questions about literary texts. Don't worry too much about these and treat them the same as any other reading question.
- You will have **three** questions in German which, as with the listening exam, could be anywhere on the paper. You won't know where they will be until you see your paper and they might not be next to each other. They will probably ask for a response in the form of a tick or a letter, etc. but you might have to write something in German. If you answer in English you won't get the mark, even if it's right. Always answer in the same language as the question.
- Read the question carefully and scan through the text for any keywords related to the question. Check the question again to make sure you are clear exactly what is being asked.
- At Foundation level, all the questions are worth 6 marks but at Higher level there will be some harder 8 mark questions at the end of the paper.
- Don't leave any questions unanswered – try to rule out any options you are sure are wrong before making a sensible guess.
- For the translation don't translate the text word for word – ensure your translation makes sense in the target language – and check you are correctly translating the tenses.
- Check carefully how many marks are available for the question. If you are asked to tick four boxes, make sure you don't tick more than four. You will lose marks for this.

The following is a guide to the types of rubrics and instructions that might be used in the listening and reading exams:

Wähle die richtige Antwort	Choose the correct answer
Hake (✓) das richtige Kästchen ab	Tick (✓) the correct box
Hake (✓) die drei richtigen Kästchen ab	Tick (✓) the three correct boxes
Ergänze die Sätze auf Deutsch	Complete the sentences in German
Höre diesen Bericht/diese Werbung/diese Gespräch an	Listen to this report/advert/conversation
Lies die Werbung/den Bericht/den Artikel	Read the advert/report/article
Lies die Information von …	Read the information from …
Schreibe zwei Details	Write two details
Schreibe den richtigen Buchstaben für jede Person	Write the correct letter for each person

Schreibe den richtigen Buchstaben	Write the correct letter
Fülle die Tabelle aus	Fill in the table
Fülle die Lücken aus	Fill in the gaps
Wer …?	Who …?
Wer hat was gesagt?	Who said what?
Beantworte die Fragen auf Deutsch	Answer the questions in German

WRITING EXAM

In the writing exam, try to bear the following points in mind:

- Check how many marks are available for each question so you know how to divide your time.
- See how many words you are recommended to write.
- Make a plan before you start writing.
- Always leave time to check your work.

Make sure you have:

- Been consistent with spellings.
- Used the correct gender for nouns.
- Used tenses appropriately.
- Used the correct endings for verbs.
- Included a range of sentence structures and vocabulary.
- Used a range of opinions and justifications.

Foundation: This exam is split into four questions.
- Question 1 – You will have to write six short sentences in German about the headings provided. Keep it short and simple!
- Question 2 – You will have to write approximately 50 words in total about the three bullet points provided. Try to write an equal amount about each bullet point and make sure you include opinions.
- Question 3 – You will have to write approximately 100 words in total about the three bullet points provided. You will be expected to use different tenses in this question.
- Question 4: Translation – You will have to translate five sentences into German.

Higher: This exam is split into three questions.
- Question 1 – You will have to write approximately 100 words in total about the three bullet points provided. You will be expected to use different tenses in this question.
- Question 2 – You will have to write approximately 150 words. There is a choice of two titles (**don't** write a response for both!). You will be expected to justify your ideas and points of view and use a range of tenses.
- Question 3: Translation – You will have to translate a paragraph into German.

Here are the sorts of rubrics and instructions that might be used in the writing exam. These examples are all in the du form but you might get some instructions in the Sie form if the examiners want you to write a piece of more formal German – e.g. a job application letter.

Wähle …	Choose …
Fülle das Formular auf Deutsch aus	Complete the form in German
Du musst einen vollständigen Satz schreiben	You must write a complete sentence
Gib Informationen und Meinungen	Give information and opinions
Schreibe ungefähr 50 Wörter auf Deutsch	Write approximately 50 words in German
Schreibe ungefähr 150 Wörter auf Deutsch	Write approximately 150 words in German
Erkläre …	Explain …
Beschreibe …	Describe …
… zu folgenden Themen	… on the following themes
Du bekommst einen Brief	You receive a letter
Beantworte auf Deutsch	Answer in German
Du musst Informationen zu folgenden Themen schreiben	You must include information on the following themes
Du kannst weitere Informationen geben	You can include more information

THE BASICS

NUMBERS

CARDINAL NUMBERS

Start by learning numbers 0–29:

0	null	8	acht	16	sechzehn	24	vierundzwanzig
1	eins	9	neun	17	siebzehn	25	fünfundzwanzig
2	zwei	10	zehn	18	achtzehn	26	sechsundzwanzig
3	drei	11	elf	19	neunzehn	27	siebenundzwanzig
4	vier	12	zwölf	20	zwanzig	28	achtundzwanzig
5	fünf	13	dreizehn	21	einundzwanzig	29	neunundzwanzig
6	sechs	14	vierzehn	22	zweiundzwanzig		
7	sieben	15	fünfzehn	23	dreiundzwanzig		

Next, make sure that you can count in tens up to 100:

10	zehn	40	vierzig	70	siebzig	100	(ein)hundert
20	zwanzig	50	fünfzig	80	achtzig		
30	dreißig	60	sechzig	90	neunzig		

To fill in the gaps between 30 and 100 use the pattern of 20–29 – e.g. 47 – siebenundvierzig, 99 – neunundneunzig.

Bigger numbers:

100	(ein)hundert
107	hundert(und)sieben
240	zweihundert(und)vierzig
1000	(ein)tausend
2300	zweitausenddreihundert
1 000 000	eine Million
2 000 000	zwei Millionen

ORDINAL NUMBERS (FIRST, SECOND, THIRD, ETC.)

Add -te to the numbers 4 to 19 and -ste to numbers from 20 onwards. Be aware of some exceptions – e.g. acht already ends in a t, so you just add -e:

1 to 1st	eins to erste
2 to 2nd	zwei to zweite

3 to 3rd	drei to dritte
4 to 4th	vier to vierte
7 to 7th	sieben to siebte
8 to 8th	acht to achte
20 to 20th	zwanzig to zwanzigste

Ordinal numbers must agree with the noun – e.g. die zweite Straße, das erste Haus.

DATES

DAYS OF THE WEEK

Montag	Monday
Dienstag	Tuesday
Mittwoch	Wednesday
Donnerstag	Thursday
Freitag	Friday
Samstag	Saturday
Sonntag	Sunday

MONTHS

Januar	January
Februar	February
März	March
April	April
Mai	May
Juni	June
Juli	July
August	August
September	September
Oktober	October
November	November
Dezember	December

SEASONS

Frühling	spring
Sommer	summer
Herbst	autumn
Winter	winter

DATES

der zweite Februar	2nd February
der erste Oktober	1st October
Heute ist der dritte April	Today is the 3rd of April

To say when a particular event is happening you can use **am** (on). Use the following pattern: for most cardinal numbers add **-ten** (up to 19) and **-sten** after 20. There are some irregular forms:

am ersten Mai
am zweiten Mai
am dritten Mai
am sechsten Mai
am siebten Mai
am achten Mai
am neunten Mai
am zwanzigsten Mai

TIME

You need to be familiar with the 12- and 24-hour clock:

2:00	zwei Uhr
14:00	vierzehn Uhr
8:00	acht Uhr
20:00	zwanzig Uhr

Minutes can be added to the hour using **nach**:

8:20	zwanzig **nach** acht
11:10	zehn **nach** elf
7:15	Viertel **nach** sieben

Minutes can be taken away from the hour using **vor**:

9:40	zwanzig **vor** zehn
6:50	zehn **vor** sieben
6:45	Viertel **vor** sieben

To say half past, German refers to the hour that is approaching:

3:30	halb vier (half an hour to four o'clock)
8:30	halb neun (half an hour to nine o'clock)

ASKING QUESTIONS

You can ask questions in two different ways:

With a question word:

wann – when
was – was
wo – where
warum – why
wie – how
wer – who
welcher – which

Was lernst du in der Schule? What do you learn at school?
Wie stressig ist die Schule? How stressful is school?

Or by verb inversion – switching the verb and subject:

Lernst du gern Informatik? Do you enjoy learning IT?
Ist Schule stressig? Is school stressful?

In German, the question word for **who** can be **wer**, **wen** or **wem** depending on the case.

Wer is the nominative form – e.g. **Wer ist das?** Who is that?
Wen is the accusative form – e.g. **Wen hast du gesehen?** Who did you see?
Wem is the dative form – e.g. **Mit wem bist du hier?** Who are you here with?

IDENTITY AND CULTURE

YOUTH CULTURE

The sub-theme of **Youth Culture** is divided into two areas. Here are some suggestions of topics to revise:

SELF AND RELATIONSHIPS

- family relationships
- friendships
- physical appearance and self-image
- fashion and trends
- celebrity culture
- problems and pressures of young people
- marriage

TECHNOLOGY AND SOCIAL MEDIA

- different types of technology – e.g. tablets, mobiles, smart watches
- advantages and disadvantages of technology
- advantages and disadvantages of social media – e.g. cyberbullying
- impact of social media
- computer games
- future of technology
- how you use technology

TRANSLATION TIPS

ENGLISH TO GERMAN

- Don't translate sentences word for word!
- Check you are correctly translating the tense required.

GERMAN TO ENGLISH

- Don't translate the text word for word – you don't need to have the same number of words in your translation as the original text has.
- Don't miss out little but important words – e.g. very, often, never.
- Make sure you translate the correct meaning of the tense – e.g. I play, I played, I will play, I would play. Sometimes keywords and phrases – like yesterday, in the future, later, usually – will help you to identify the tense.

Beschreibe deine Familie.
Describe your family.

Ich habe eine Schwester, die Sophie heißt. Ich verstehe mich gut mit ihr, weil wir die gleiche Musik mögen. Sie ist immer lustig. Außerdem habe ich einen Bruder, der älter als ich ist. Ich denke, dass meine Eltern zu streng sind, und das ist wirklich ärgerlich.

I have a sister called Sophie. I get on well with her because we like the same music. She is always funny. I also have a brother who is older than me. I think that my parents are too strict and that's really annoying.

Was hast du letztes Wochenende mit deinen Freunden gemacht?
What did you do with your friends last weekend?

Letzten Freitag bin ich mit meinen Schulfreunden ins Kino gegangen. Nach dem Film sind wir in ein Restaurant gegangen. Wir haben Pizza gegessen.

Last Friday I went to the cinema with my friends from school. After the film we went to a restaurant. We ate pizza.

Findest du Mode wichtig?
Is fashion important to you?

Ja, natürlich. Ich finde Models und Prominente inspirierend und ich kaufe gern neue Kleidung. Später möchte ich in der Modeindustrie arbeiten.

Yes, of course. I'm inspired by models and celebrities and I love buying new clothes. Later I'd like to work in the fashion industry.

Wer ist dein Lieblingsstar? Warum?
Who is your favourite star? Why?

Ich bewundere Ed Sheeran, weil er gute Texte schreibt. Letztes Jahr habe ich ihn live gesehen. Es war toll!

I admire Ed Sheeran because he writes good lyrics. Last year I saw him live. It was great!

Wie würdest du deinen idealen Freund/deine ideale Freundin beschreiben?
How would you describe your ideal girlfriend/boyfriend?

Er/sie würde einen guten Beruf haben und reich und großzügig sein. Meiner Meinung nach ist es wichtig, einen guten Sinn für Humor zu haben.
He/she would have a good job and be rich and generous. In my opinion, it's important to have a good sense of humour.

Try to use a variety of vocabulary and sentence structures.

There's no need (and you won't have enough time) to describe the colour of every member of your family's hair, eyes, etc. The vocabulary you will be using could become really repetitive.

It's easy for this topic to become too descriptive and rely mainly on present tense. Try to include some opinions – What do you think of different family members? How do you get on? Why?

Say what you did/are going to do with your family to show off your use of different tenses.

GRAMMAR

Possessive adjectives

Possessive adjectives show ownership – e.g. my, his. To use the correct possessive adjective you need to know:

1. Which one is needed – e.g. **mein, dein, sein.**
2. What gender the noun is – e.g. **meine Schwester ist ..., mein Bruder ist ...**
3. The case your noun is going to be in.

Possessive adjectives include:

mein – my
dein – your (informal)
sein – his/its
ihr – her/their
unser – our
euer – your (plural)
Ihr – your (formal)

EXAM TASK

Translate the sentences into English:

1. Meine Tante ist lustig, sympathisch und sportlich.
2. Als ich jünger war, hatte ich viele Freunde.
3. Er versteht sich gut mit seiner Schwester.
4. Wie kommst du mit deiner Familie aus?

Have you translated all the information? Does the sentence you have written make sense in English?

SELF AND RELATIONSHIPS

Ich interessiere mich für Mode.	I am interested in fashion.
Ich trage lieber Markenkleidung.	I prefer wearing designer clothes.
Es ist mein Ziel, berühmt zu warden.	It's my aim to become famous.
Ich lese gern Modezeitschriften.	I like reading fashion magazines.
Ich möchte in der Zukunft heiraten.	I would like to get married in the future.
Meiner Meinung nach ist es sehr wichtig, eine Familie zu haben.	In my opinion, having a family is very important.
Es scheint mir, dass modische Kleidung zu teuer ist.	It seems to me that fashionable clothes are too expensive.
Mein Traumpartner/meine Traumpartnerin würde ... sein/machen/haben.	My dream girlfriend/boyfriend would be …/do …/have …
Ich kann ihm/ihr alles erzählen.	I can tell him/her everything.
Es gibt manchmal Streit.	There are sometimes arguments.
Meine Eltern sind zu streng.	My parents are too strict.
Ich kann mich immer auf meine Freunde verlassen.	I can always count on my friends.
Wir streiten selten.	We rarely argue.
Wir chatten im Internet.	We chat on the internet.
Ich sehe wie meine Schwester aus.	I look like my sister.
Meine Freunde sagen, dass ich einen guten Sinn für Humor habe.	My friends say I've got a good sense of humour.
Heutzutage haben junge Leute viele Probleme.	Young people today have lots of problems.
Popstars können einen schlechten Einfluss auf junge Leute haben.	Popstars can be a bad influence on young people.
Ich habe vor, mit meinen Freunden zusammen zu wohnen.	I intend to live with my friends.
Ich verstehe mich gut mit meiner Schwester.	I get on well with my sister.
Ich streite mich oft mit meinen Eltern.	I often argue with my parents.
Er/sie kritisiert mich immer.	He/she criticises me all the time.

Use and adapt expressions like these
in your speaking and writing exams to
access higher marks.

EXAM TASK

Beschreibe das Foto./Was passiert auf diesem Foto?

Dieses Foto zeigt eine Gruppe von Studenten. Sie sind in der Schule und tragen
keine Uniform. Ich glaube, dass sie über das Mädchen, das alleine ist, sprechen.
Ich denke, dass sie das Opfer von Schulmobbing ist. Meiner Meinung nach ist sie
traurig, weil sie keine Freunde hat.

In this photo there is a group of students. They are at school and they are not
wearing uniform. I think they are talking about the girl who is alone. I think she
is the victim of school bullying. In my opinion, she is sad because she doesn't have
any friends.

Now can you answer these questions yourself?

- Wie sind deine Freunde? What are your friends like?
- Freunde sind wichtiger als Familie. Was sagst du dazu? Friends are more
  important than family. What do you think?
- Was wirst du nächstes Wochenende mit deiner Familie machen? What are you
  going to do with your family next weekend?

TECHNOLOGY AND SOCIAL MEDIA

Was ist deine Lieblingswebseite und warum?
What is your favourite website and why?

> Ich benutze oft Google, um mir mit Hausaufgaben und Schulprojekten zu helfen.
> I often use Google to help with homework and school projects.

Wofür benutzt du Social-Media-Seiten?
What do you use social media for?

> Ich benutze gern Social-Media-Seiten, um meine Gedanken zu teilen. Ich bleibe in Kontakt mit Freunden überall auf der Welt und sehe gern ihre Fotos.
> I love using social media to share my thoughts. I stay in contact with my friends around the world and like to see their photos.

Was sind die negativen Aspekte von Technologie?
What are the negative aspects of technology?

> Technologie kann gefährlich sein. Man kann Leute online treffen, die über ihr Alter oder ihren Namen lügen können. Man muss vorsichtig sein, mit wem man redet.
> Technology can be dangerous. You can meet people online who can lie about their age or their name. You must be careful who you speak to.

Wofür hast du gestern Technologie benutzt?
What did you use technology for yesterday?

> Ich habe Fotos und Videos hochgeladen. Dann habe ich einen Blog gelesen. Ich habe meine Hausaufgaben am Computer gemacht. Ich habe auch einen Film heruntergeladen.
> I uploaded photos and videos. Then I read a blog. I did my homework on the computer. I also downloaded a film.

Brauchst du ein Handy?
Do you need a mobile phone?

Für die meisten Jugendliche ist ein Handy nötig. Persönlich könnte ich ohne mein Handy nicht leben, weil es so nützlich ist. Ich bin wirklich abhängig!
A mobile phone is necessary for most young people. Personally I couldn't live without my phone because it's so useful. I am really addicted!

Hopefully you should have a lot to say about this topic!

You may be so in love with technology that you can't think of any disadvantages or problems, but it's important that you can offer a range of opinions. Learn a variety of ways of giving opinions – e.g. **es ist** (it is), **ich denke, dass** (I think that), **ich finde, dass** (I find that), **meiner Meinung nach** (in my opinion), **was mich betrifft** (as far as I'm concerned), **es wird oft gesagt, dass** (it's often said that) – and try to use a range of adjectives. Examiners can get fed up of everything being **interessant** or **langweilig**.

EXAM TASK

Answer the questions in English.

Mobbing[1] bekommt über das Internet eine neue Dimension. Es gab eine Cybermobbing-Studie mit mehr als 10 000 Schülern, Eltern und Lehrern. Immer öfter werden zum Mobben internetfähige Handys benutzt, die laut der Studie zwei Drittel aller Schüler besitzen[2]. Jeder sechste Schüler in Deutschland hatte schon einmal ein Problem mit Mobbing im Internet. Das Problem ist am schlimmsten in der Gruppe der 14- bis 16-jährigen, aber es beginnt schon in der Grundschule.

Bei den Opfern[3] bringt das oft Probleme mit sich wie:

- Konzentrationsprobleme
- schlechte Noten in der Schule
- Kopf- und Magenschmerzen
- Angst

[1] bullying
[2] to own
[3] victims

1. How many students own a mobile phone? (1 mark)
2. How many young people have had a problem with cyberbullying? (1 mark)
   a. 6000
   b. 1 in 6
   c. 1 in 2
3. Write **three** ways in which victims suffer. (3 marks)

Watch out for distractors (annoying words the examiners put in to try to trick you)! There are several numbers and statistics mentioned in this text.

TECHNOLOGY AND SOCIAL MEDIA

Meine Eltern sagen, dass ich zu viel Zeit im Internet verbringe.	My parents say I spend too much time on the internet.
Ich finde das Internet sehr nützlich.	I think the internet is very useful.
Meine Eltern kaufen oft Kleidung im Internet.	My parents often buy clothes online.
Ich lade Musik mit meinem Handy herunter.	I download music with my mobile phone.
Letztes Wochenende habe ich viele Urlaubsfotos hochgeladen.	Last weekend I uploaded lots of holiday photos.
Ich treffe gern neue Leute online.	I like meeting people online.
Technologie spielt eine wichtige Rolle im Alltag von Jugendlichen.	Technology plays an important role in the life of young people.
Meiner Meinung nach ist das Leben einfacher mit Technologie.	In my opinion, life is easier with technology.
Meine Mutter denkt, dass Social-Media-Seiten eine Zeitverschwendung sind.	My mum thinks social media sites are a waste of time.
Man kann internetsüchtig warden.	You can become addicted to the internet.
Cybermobbing ist ein großes Problem.	Cyberbullying is a big problem.
Es gibt viele Internet-Betrügereien.	There are lots of internet scams.
Handys sind in einem Notfall sehr nützlich.	Mobile phones are very useful in an emergency.
Handys verursachen viele Autounfälle.	Mobile phones cause many car accidents.
Ich bin abends oft zwei Stunden online, um mit meinen Freunden zu chatten.	I'm often online for two hours in the evening to chat with friends.

Negatives

Negative sentences are easy to form in German. Try to include some in your work – e.g. Ich spiele keine Computerspiele.

- Nicht means not and is usually used to negate a verb – e.g. Technologie ist **nicht** wichtig in meinem Leben.
- Kein is usually used to negate a noun – e.g.:
  Ich habe **kein** Handy.
  Es gibt **keinen** Internetzugang in meinem Dorf.
- Watch out for other words that can make a sentence negative – e.g.:
  nie – never
  nicht mehr – no longer
  nichts – nothing
  weder ... noch ... – neither ... nor ...
  noch nicht – not yet
  niemand – no one
  nirgendwo – nowhere

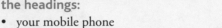

EXAM TASK

Write a full sentence in German for each of the headings:

- your mobile phone
- computer games
- social media
- technology – your opinion
- music
- the internet – a disadvantage

There's no need to write a really complicated sentence. A simple sentence can score full marks even if it has some minor errors. There isn't just one correct answer – e.g. for the first bullet point you could say:

Mein Handy ist klein. My mobile phone is small.

Or you could even use a negative sentence:

Ich habe kein Handy. I haven't got a mobile phone.

IDENTITY AND CULTURE

LIFESTYLE

The sub-theme of **Lifestyle** is divided into two areas. Here are some suggestions of topics to revise:

HEALTH AND FITNESS

- healthy eating
- health issues – e.g. stress, illnesses
- unhealthy lifestyle – e.g. drugs, alcohol, smoking
- sports and exercise
- benefits of a healthy lifestyle

ENTERTAINMENT AND LEISURE

- music
- cinema
- television
- shopping
- eating out
- social activities and hobbies
- work–life balance

REMEMBER:

It's really important to keep revising questions – remember that you will have to answer unpredictable questions in your speaking exam and you will also have to ask a present tense question in the role play. You also have to talk about events in the past, present and future tense in the photo card discussion and the conversation. It's really important that you are able to recognise questions in different tenses – e.g. Was machst du normalerweise? (What do you usually do?), Was hast du gestern gemacht? (What did you do yesterday?), Was wirst du nächste Woche machen? (What will you do next week?) Listen out for time phrases – e.g. nächste Woche (next week), gestern (yesterday), etc. – that will help you answer in the correct tense.

HEALTH AND FITNESS

Was machst du, um fit zu bleiben?
What do you do to keep fit?

Ich mache viel, um fit zu bleiben. Ich treibe drei- oder viermal pro Woche Sport und ich esse gesund. Nach meinen Prüfungen werde ich jeden Tag schwimmen gehen.
I do lots of things to keep fit. I do sport three or four times a week and I eat healthily. After my exams, I will go swimming every day.

Was machst du lieber – Sport treiben oder Sportsendungen sehen? Warum?
Which do you prefer – doing sport or watching sports programmes? Why?

Ich bin sehr sportlich und bin Mitglied in der Fußball- und Hockeymannschaft in der Schule. Jedoch sehe ich auch gern Fußballspiele im Stadion oder im Fernsehen.
I'm a very sporty person and I am a member of the school football and hockey teams. However, I also like watching football matches at the stadium or on TV.

Was ist schlecht für deine Gesundheit?
What is bad for your health?

Man muss nicht rauchen, weil es ernste Krankenheiten wie Lungenkrebs verursachen kann. Alkohol trinken ist auch schlecht für die Gesundheit. Leider fühlen sich junge Leute oft unter Druck, auf Partys zu trinken.
You mustn't smoke because it can cause serious illnesses like lung cancer. Drinking alcohol is bad for your health as well. Unfortunately, lots of young people feel under pressure to drink at parties.

Was wirst du in der Zukunft machen, um gesünder zu essen?
What will you do in the future to eat more healthily?

Ich werde mehr Obst essen und fettiges Essen vermeiden. Ich werde versuchen, täglich ein gesundes Frühstück zu essen. Ich werde auch weniger Schokolade essen, obwohl ich das schwer finden werde.
I am going to eat more fruit and avoid fatty food. I will try to eat a good breakfast every day. I will eat less chocolate, although I'll find that difficult.

Was hast du letztes Wochenende gemacht, um fit zu bleiben?
What did you do last weekend to keep fit?

Samstagmorgen habe ich Tennis mit meinem Bruder gespielt. Dann sind wir ins Sportzentrum gegangen, um zu schwimmen. Es war anstrengend!
Saturday morning, I played tennis with my brother. Then we went to the sports centre to go swimming. It was tiring!

GRAMMAR

Conjunctions

Some conjunctions like **weil** (because) change the word order in German. It's a 'verb scarer' – i.e. it scares the verb to the end of the sentence.

- Ich esse oder trinke keine Milchprodukte. Ich habe eine Laktose-Intoleranz. I don't eat or drink any dairy products. I have a lactose intolerance.
- Ich esse oder trinke keine Milchprodukte, **weil** ich eine Laktose-Intoleranz habe. I don't eat or drink any dairy products, because I have a lactose intolerance.

Some other common ones are:

bevor – before
da/weil – because
obwohl – although
wenn – when/if
damit – so that

Answer the questions in English.

EXAM TASK

Die meisten **Jugendlichen** sind heutzutage knapp 15 Jahre alt, wenn sie ihr erstes Glas **Alkohol trinken**. Im Jahr 2004 lag das Durchschnittsalter noch bei 14 Jahren. Die Schlagzeile in den Zeitungen „Jugendliche trinken immer früher Alkohol" stimmt also nicht.

Viele junge Erwachsene im Alter zwischen 18 und 25 Jahren haben in ihrem Leben schon einmal Alkohol getrunken, nämlich 96 Prozent. Bei den 12- bis 17-jährigen Jugendlichen sieht das schon anders aus: 69 Prozent von ihnen berichten über Erfahrungen mit Alkohol. 31 Prozent haben noch nie in ihrem Leben Alkohol getrunken.

Die Definition von regelmäßigem **Alkoholkonsum** ist „mindestens einmal pro Woche". 38 Prozent der jungen Erwachsenen (18 bis 25 Jahre) trinken regelmäßig – normalerweise auf Partys.

1. What is the text about?
2. What does the figure 96% refer to?
3. What does the figure 31% refer to?
4. How is the word 'regularly' defined in the article?

Question 1 is a new style of question which you can expect to see in your listening and reading exams. Try to identify some keywords (we have highlighted some in bold in this article to help you – unfortunately that won't happen in the real thing!). Make sure you read the whole text before answering the question. Don't be distracted by a few keywords in the text – e.g. **Zeitungen, Partys.**

HEALTH AND FITNESS

Ich sollte mehr Wasser trinken.	I should drink more water.
Ich werde nie rauchen.	I am never going to smoke.
Ich werde mehr Obst und Gemüse essen.	I am going to eat more fruit and vegetables.
Ich möchte weniger Süßigkeiten essen.	I would like to eat fewer sweets.
Ich möchte fit sein.	I would like to be fit.
Wenn ich mehr Geld hätte, würde ich Bioprodukte kaufen.	If I had more money, I would buy organic products.
Ich sollte früher ins Bett gehen.	I should go to bed earlier.
Als ich jünger war, habe ich oft Fast Food gegessen.	When I was younger, I often ate fast food.
Man sollte fünf Portionen Obst und Gemüse am Tag essen.	You should eat five portions of fruit and vegetables a day.
Ich esse selten Frühstück.	I rarely eat breakfast.
Eine ausgewogene Ernährung ist wichtig.	A balanced diet is important.
Ich treibe zwei- bis dreimal pro Woche Sport.	I do sport two to three times a week.
Ich esse nie zwischen den Mahlzeiten.	I never eat between meals.
Ich habe noch nie Alkohol getrunken.	I've never drunk alcohol.
Man sollte nicht zu viel Fett, Zucker oder Salz essen.	You shouldn't eat too much fat, sugar or salt.
Ich rauche nicht, weil es ungesund ist.	I don't smoke, because it's unhealthy.
Man kann leicht süchtig warden.	You can easily get addicted.
Es gibt mehrere Risiken.	There are several risks.

Use of seit.

Remember that **seit** can be used with the present tense in German to say how long you have been doing something for.

- Ich spiele **seit** sechs Jahren Basketball. I have been playing basketball for six years (and still do!).
- Ich bin **seit** drei Jahren Vegetarier. I've been a vegetarian for three years (and still am!).

EXAM TASK

In the role play you will have to ask a question, use more than one tense and respond to an unexpected question! Here are some examples of the prompts you might see:

- Say what you do to stay healthy.
- Ask your friend a question about sport.
- Give your opinion on healthy eating.
- Say what sport you did yesterday.
- Ask your friend what food he/she likes to eat.
- Say what you will do next week to stay healthy.

There are lots of different questions you could ask about sport.

You could keep it general – e.g. **Treibst du gern Sport?** (Do you like sport?) **Magst du Fußball?** (Do you like football?)

Or be more specific – e.g. **Wann spielst du Tennis?** (When do you play tennis?) **Mit wem spielst du Basketball?** (Who do you play basketball with?)

Watch out for 'trigger' words which mean your response needs to be in a different tense – e.g. yesterday, next week.

ENTERTAINMENT AND LEISURE

Was machst du in deiner Freizeit?
What do you do in your free time?

Im Moment habe ich nicht viel Freizeit wegen meiner Prüfungen, aber Schwimmen ist, was ich wirklich liebe. Ich gehe mindestens dreimal pro Woche ins Schwimmbad. Zu Hause sehe ich fern und spiele auf meinem Handy.
At the moment I don't have much free time because of my exams, but swimming is what I really love. I go to the swimming pool at least three times a week. At home I watch TV and play on my mobile phone.

Sind Hobbys wichtig für junge Leute?
Are hobbies important for young people?

Ja, natürlich. Heutzutage haben junge Leute viele Prüfungen, deswegen sind Hobbys sehr wichtig, um sich zu entspannen.
Yes, of course. These days, young people have lots of exams so hobbies are really important for relaxing.

Welche Freizeitaktivität möchtest du in der Zukunft machen?
What leisure activity would you like to try in the future?

Ich möchte Snowboard fahren, weil ich es noch nie gemacht habe. Mein Bruder sagt, dass es aufregend ist.
I'd like to snowboard because I've never tried it. My brother told me it's exciting.

Was hast du letztes Wochenende gemacht?
What did you do last weekend?

Samstagmorgen habe ich lange geschlafen. Nach dem Mittagessen bin ich in die Stadt gegangen. Samstagabend bin ich mit meinen Freunden ins Kino gegangen. Wir haben eine Komödie gesehen und es war wirklich lustig. Saturday morning, I had a lie in. After lunch I went to town. Saturday evening I went to the cinema with my friends. We watched a comedy and it was really funny.

Siehst du lieber Filme zu Hause oder im Kino? Warum?
Do you prefer watching films at home or at the cinema? Why?

Das Kino ist sehr teuer, deswegen sehe ich lieber Filme zu Hause. Mein Wohnzimmer ist sehr bequem und ich kann essen, was ich will. The cinema is very expensive so I prefer watching films at home. My living room is very comfortable and I can eat whatever I want.

Try to develop your answers as much as possible by adding extra detail wherever you can – e.g. to Ich gehe ins Kino ...

- Add who with – Ich gehe **mit meinen Freunden** ins Kino.
- Add a time phrase – Ich gehe **am Samstag** mit meinen Freunden ins Kino.
- Add an opinion – Ich gehe am Samstag mit meinen Freunden ins Kino. **Es ist prima.**
- Add a justification – Ich gehe am Samstag mit meinen Freunden ins Kino. Es ist prima, **weil das Kino modern ist.**
- Add a different tense – Ich gehe am Samstag mit meinen Freunden ins Kino. Es ist prima, weil das Kino modern ist. **Letzten Samstag habe ich eine Komödie gesehen.**

EXAM TASK

Match the name to the statement.
Andreas: Ich bin ein Fan von FIFA und meine Eltern kaufen mir das Spiel jedes Jahr zu meinem Geburtstag. Dann beschweren sie sich immer, dass ich zu viel Zeit mit Spielen verbringe!

Nina: Computerspiele? Ja, ich bin süchtig. Ich spiele lieber mit meinen Freunden, weil ich nicht gern allein spiele. Wir diskutieren gemeinsam, während wir spielen.

Timo: Ich spiele, um mich zu entspannen. Ich spiele mit meinem Bruder und ich gewinnne oft. Ich spiele nachts, obwohl meine Eltern glauben, dass ich schlafe.

Who do you think would say the following? Andreas, Nina or Timo?

1. I play to relax.
2. I am addicted to games.
3. I play with my friends.
4. My parents always complain.
5. I play it at night.

Be careful with statement 4 as both Andreas and Timo mention their parents!

ENTERTAINMENT AND LEISURE

Es ist wichtig, Hobbys zu haben.	It's important to have hobbies.
Meiner Meinung nach ist das Leben besser, wenn man viele Freizeitaktivitäten hat.	In my opinion, life is better when you have lots of leisure activities.
Letztes Jahr hatte ich mehr Freizeit.	Last year I had more free time.
Wenn ich keine Hausaufgaben habe, gehe ich gern mit Freunden aus.	When I don't have homework, I like going out with my friends.
In meiner Freizeit spiele ich Fußball, weil es meine Leidenschaft ist.	During my free time I play football because it's my passion.
Ich spiele gern am Computer, weil es mich entspannt.	I love playing on the computer because it relaxes me.
Als ich jünger war, habe ich Gitarre gespielt, aber jetzt habe ich nicht genug Zeit.	When I was younger, I played the guitar but now I don't have enough time.
Wenn ich keine Schularbeit habe, spiele ich Computerspiele, um mich zu entspannen.	If I don't have any schoolwork, I play computer games to relax.
Nach meinen Prüfungen möchte ich viele neue Aktivitäten ausprobieren.	After my exams, I would like to try lots of new activities.
Hobbys sind eine gute Chance, neue Freunde kennenzulernen.	Hobbies are a good opportunity to make new friends.
Ich höre gern Ed Sheeran, weil er eine gute Stimme hat.	I like Ed Sheeran, because he has a good voice.
Es gibt nicht genug Konzerte in meiner Stadt.	There aren't enough concerts in my town.

GRAMMAR

Adding detail

Try to include more detail in your sentences by using time phrases and adverbs of time and place:

immer – always
manchmal – sometimes
ab und zu – now and then
selten – rarely
letzte Woche – last week
nächste Woche – next week
jeden Tag – every day
am Freitag – on Friday
freitags – on Fridays
abends – in the evening

EXAM TASK

Translate these sentences into German:

1. Last week I went shopping in town.
2. Next weekend I am going to the cinema with my family.
3. What is your favourite TV programme?
4. I can't go out tomorrow because I have lots of homework.

Remember:

- Don't translate word for word.
- Don't leave any gaps.
- Watch out for different tenses.
- Be careful with negatives.

IDENTITY AND CULTURE

CUSTOMS AND TRADITIONS

The sub-theme of **Customs and Traditions** is divided into two areas. Here are some suggestions of topics to revise:

FOOD AND DRINK
- party food and drink
- regional specialities
- eating habits
- cultural traditions
- food and drink for special occasions
- eating out

FESTIVALS AND CELEBRATIONS
- annual festivals and holidays
- birthdays
- national events
- regional events
- music festivals
- celebrating family occasions

REMEMBER:
- You need to use a variety of tenses in your written and spoken German.
- Use your verb tables to help you when you are planning your work.
- Remember to use the correct verb form – this tells the examiner who the sentence is about. You need to use the ich form to talk about yourself, but you need to learn other verb forms as well so that you can talk about other people.
- Try to include more detail by adding time expressions where possible – e.g. heute (today), jeden Tag (every day), diese Woche (this week), normalerweise (usually), gestern Abend (yesterday evening), letzte Woche (last week), vor zwei Monaten (two months ago), nächstes Jahr (next year), in der Zukunft (in the future).

FOOD AND DRINK

Kochst du gern? Warum (nicht)?
Do you like cooking? Why (not)?

Als ich jünger war, habe ich gern Kuchen mit meinem Vater gebacken. Jetzt mache ich nur Butterbrote. Ich sehe gern Kochsendungen im Fernsehen, aber ich habe nicht genug Zeit, um zu kochen.
When I was younger, I liked making cakes with my father. Now I only make sandwiches! I like watching cookery programmes on TV but I don't have enough time to cook.

Wann bist du zum letzten Mal in ein Restaurant gegangen?
When did you last go to a restaurant?

Ich bin letztes Wochenende mit meiner Familie in ein italienisches Restaurant gegangen. Ich habe Pizza mit Hähnchen gegessen, und als Nachtisch hatte ich Erdbeereis. Das Essen war lecker und ich möchte wieder dort essen.
I went to an Italian restaurant with my family last weekend. I ate a pizza with chicken, and for dessert I had strawberry ice cream. The food was delicious and I'd like to eat there again.

Ist es wichtig, regionale Gerichte im Urlaub zu essen? Warum (nicht)?
Is it important to eat regional dishes on holiday? Why (not)?

Nach meiner Ansicht sollten Touristen die lokale Kultur respektieren. Ich glaube, dass es nötig ist, traditionelle Gerichte zu probieren. Außerdem sind Touristen-Restaurants oft sehr teuer.
In my opinion, tourists should respect the culture of the region. I think it's essential to try local dishes. Furthermore, tourist restaurants are often very expensive.

Was wäre deine ideale Mahlzeit?
What would your ideal meal be?

Ich würde in einem Restaurant am Strand in der Karibik essen. Ich würde regionale Gerichte probieren und alkoholfreie Cocktails trinken.
I would eat in a restaurant on the beach in the Caribbean. I would try local specialities and I would drink alcohol-free cocktails.

Wie findest du Fertiggerichte?
What do you think of ready meals?

Ich esse ab und zu Fertiggerichte, zum Beispiel Tiefkühlpizza, weil ich nicht gern koche. Ich finde Fertiggerichte schnell und praktisch, aber ich esse lieber hausgemachte Mahlzeiten.
I eat ready meals from time to time, for example frozen pizzas, because I don't like cooking. I think ready meals are quick and practical but I prefer to eat home-cooked meals.

You may have to talk or write about the sort of food and drink you normally have at a celebration – e.g. a birthday party. Show the examiner that you're hungry for success by showing off some different tenses and use some intensifiers to improve your work.

GRAMMAR

Intensifiers

It's important to give a range of opinions in your speaking and writing tasks. Try to use a range of adjectives so everything isn't **gut** or **interessant** and use intensifiers with adjectives to add emphasis:

sehr – very
zu – too
viel – much
ganz/ziemlich – quite
ein wenig – a little
wirklich – really
ein bisschen – a bit
einfach – simply
gar nicht/überhaupt nicht – not at all

EXAM TASK

Answer the questions about this literary text in English.

Deutschland liegt in der Mitte des modernen Europas – das merkt man auch an unseren Lieblingsgerichten. Heute essen wir genauso gern Pizza und Pasta, Döner und Gyros wie traditionelle Rinderrouladen und Sauerkraut. Zuwanderer aus südlichen und östlichen Ländern brachten über viele Jahre Familienrezepte und Essgewohnheiten mit.

Kochen ist am besten mit einer Familie, die zusammen kocht und isst. Früher haben Kinder das Kochen einfach durch Zuschauen zu Hause gelernt, heute brauchen wir Kochschulen. Ich würde das gern ändern.

Grundregeln:

- Zeit ist die wichtigste Zutat.
- Salz und Zucker gehören immer zusammen.

1. How is Germany described in the first line?
2. Where have people come from to live in Germany?
3. How would he like the book to be used?
4. What does he say is the most important ingredient?

There will be two extracts from literary texts in your reading exam. Treat them just like any other reading comprehension task. Don't worry if you can't understand every single word.

FOOD AND DRINK

Kochen ist nicht mein Ding.	Cooking is not my thing.
Wenn ich Zeit hätte, würde ich öfter kochen.	If I had the time, I would cook more often.
Heutzutage haben wir oft nicht genug Zeit oder Energie, um Essen von Grund auf zu kochen.	These days, we don't always have the time or energy to cook a meal from scratch.
Fertiggerichte sind kalorienreich und enthalten zu viel Zucker und Salz.	Ready meals are high in calories and contain too much sugar and salt.
Mein Lieblingsessen ist Hähnchen mit Pommes.	My favourite meal is chicken and chips.
Jedes Land bietet kulinarische Spezialitäten.	Every country has its own culinary specialities.
Eine „handyfreie Zeit" beim Essen ist eine gute Idee.	It's a good idea to 'ban' mobile phones whilst eating.
Ich probiere gern Essen aus verschiedenen Ländern.	I like trying food from different countries.
Ich esse fast alles, aber ich kann Pilze nicht leiden.	I eat almost everything, but I can't stand mushrooms.
Nach meiner Ansicht ist es altmodisch, zusammen als Familie zu essen.	In my opinion, eating dinner together as a family is old-fashioned.
Eine gemeinsame Mahlzeit schafft Zeit für Gespräche.	A shared meal creates time for conversation.
Mein Bruder hat viele Allergien.	My brother has lots of allergies.
Ich sehe gern Kochsendungen wie Masterchef.	I enjoy watching cookery shows like *Masterchef*.
Ich würde sehr gern in einem Restaurant mit Michelin-Stern essen.	I would really like to eat in a Michelin-starred restaurant.

Schreiben Sie einen Artikel für eine Webseite. Sie müssen Informationen zu folgenden Themen schreiben:

- wie das Restaurant war
- was Sie gegessen und getrunken haben
- wie Sie es gefunden haben und warum

Schreiben Sie ungefähr 100 Wörter auf Deutsch.

Remember:
- Try to stick closely to the recommended word count.
- There is nothing to be gained by writing more than the recommended word count – in fact, your work may become less accurate and you may run out of time for other questions.
- Divide your time equally between all three bullet points.
- Draft a brief plan before you start writing.
- Leave enough time to check your work otherwise you may lose marks for lack of accuracy.

GRAMMAR

Relative pronouns

- Relative pronouns are used to refer back to a noun from a previous part of the sentence. In English the words **who**, **which** or **what** are usually used.
- In German, relative pronouns send the verb to the end of the sentence. The pronoun you need to use depends on the gender of the noun you are referring back to:

  - der – Der Tisch, der in der Ecke ist, ist viel zu klein. The table, which is in the corner, is much too small.
  - die – Die Bäckerei, die in der Stadt ist, ist toll! The bakery, which is in town, is great!
  - das – Mein Lieblingsrestaurant, das Nandos heißt, ist in der Stadtmitte. My favourite restaurant, which is called Nandos, is in the town centre.

- **Was** and **wo** can also be used as relative pronouns.
- Remember that the verb in the subordinate clause goes to the end of the sentence:

  - Ich weiß nicht, was ich kochen **werde**. I don't know what I will cook.
  - Ich reise gerne nach Polen, wo man leckere Kuchen kaufen **kann**. I like visiting Poland, where you can buy delicious cakes.

Möhren-Kartoffel-
Eintopf mit
Bockwurst € 6,50

Flammkuchen
"Herzhaft" € 7,80

Hausgemachte
Champignoncreme
€ 4,20

FESTIVALS AND CELEBRATIONS

Was ist dein Lieblingsfest? Warum?
What is your favourite festival? Why?

Mein Lieblingsfest ist Silvester, weil man die ganze Nacht aufbleiben kann. Letztes Jahr um Mitternacht haben wir die Feuerwerke gesehen. Es hat mir wirklich gut gefallen.
My favourite festival is New Year's Eve because you can stay up all night. Last year we watched the fireworks at midnight. I really liked it.

Was hast du letztes Jahr an Halloween gemacht?
What did you do last year for Halloween?

Ich habe mich als Geist verkleidet und mein Bruder hatte Angst. Es war sehr lustig!
I dressed up as a ghost and my brother was scared. It was very funny!

Wie findest du traditionelle Feste?
What do you think of traditional festivals?

Ich finde diese traditionellen Feste sehr wichtig, weil wir Zeit mit der Familie verbringen. Es gibt oft leckeres Essen.
I think these traditional festivals are important because we spend time with the family. There's often tasty food.

Was wirst du an deinem nächsten Geburtstag machen?
What will you do for your next birthday?

Ich werde mit meinen besten Freunden und meiner Familie feiern. Meine Mutter wird einen Geburtstagskuchen für mich backen und meine Schwester wird eine Party organisieren. Ich freue mich schon darauf.
I will celebrate my birthday with my best friends and my family. My mum will make me a birthday cake and my sister will organise a party. I'm already looking forward to it.

Gibt es ein Fest, das du besuchen möchtest?
Is there a festival that you would like to go to?

Ich bin nie bei einem Musikfest gewesen. Nach meinen Prüfungen möchte ich mit meinen Freunden zum Musikfest gehen. Wir werden zelten und unsere Lieblingsgruppen sehen.
I've never been to a music festival. After my exams, I would like to go to a festival with my friends. We will go camping and we will see our favourite groups.

GRAMMAR

Modal verbs

When using modal verbs to talk about events in the past you usually need to use the imperfect tense.

Here are the ich forms:

ich konnte – I could
ich durfte – I was allowed to
ich sollte – I was supposed to
ich musste – I had to
ich wollte – I wanted to

- **Ich durfte** zum Musikfest gehen. I was allowed to go to the music festival.
- **Ich musste** viel Geld mitnehmen. I had to take a lot of money.
- **Ich wollte** meine Lieblingsgruppe sehen. I wanted to see my favourite group.

EXAM TASK

Translate the following paragraph into English:

Ich war letzte Woche bei einem Musikfest in München. Es hat viel Spaß gemacht, weil ich mit meinen Freunden da war. Wir haben stundenlang getanzt und neue Freunde aus ganz Deutschland kennengelernt. Die Musik war klasse und ich habe ein T-Shirt als Souvenir gekauft. Jetzt verstehe ich, warum Musikfeste so beliebt sind.

The translation into English is the last question on the reading exam and is worth 6 marks – this is only 2.5% of the whole GCSE so don't spend more time on it than you would on any other question on the reading paper.

FESTIVALS AND CELEBRATIONS

Normalerweise feiere ich meinen Geburtstag mit meinen Freunden.	Usually, I celebrate my birthday with my friends.
Meine Oma kocht immer etwas Traditionelles.	My grandma always cooks something traditional.
Nach dem Essen bekomme ich meine Geschenke.	After the meal I get my presents.
Ich hatte Glück, weil ich viele Geschenke bekommen habe.	I was lucky because I received a lot of presents.
Wir hatten eine große Party und es gab Feuerwerke.	We had a big party and there were fireworks.
Jedes Jahr schicke ich viele Weihnachtskarten.	Every year I send lots of Christmas cards.
Wir haben viel gegessen.	We ate a lot.
Das Festival wurde 1986 gegründet.	The festival was founded in 1986.
Andererseits sind viele Festivals zu kommerzialisiert geworden.	On the other hand, many festivals have become too commercial.
Traditionen sind nicht sehr wichtig.	Traditions aren't very important.
Man kann viele verschiedene Bands günstig sehen.	You can see lots of bands for a reasonable price.
Es gibt eine tolle Stimmung.	There's a great atmosphere.
Oft wird zu viel Alkohol getrunken und das verursacht Probleme.	Too much alcohol is often drunk and that causes problems.
Es gibt viel Abfall und das ist schlecht für die Umwelt.	There is lots of rubbish and that's bad for the environment.

Answering conversation questions on each topic in writing is good practice for your writing exam.

Use and adapt the useful phrases on page 46 to help you answer the following. Remember to use a variety of tenses and to include more than one piece of information where possible. Can you justify your opinions?

- Feierst du lieber mit Familie oder Freunden? Warum? Do you prefer celebrating your birthday with family or friends? Why?
- Geburtstagspartys sind teuer. Was sagst du dazu? Birthday parties are expensive. What do you think?
- Beschreibe deine Lieblingsparty. Describe your favourite birthday party.
- Wie wäre deine Traumparty? What would your ideal party be like?
- Sind Traditionen wichtig? Warum (nicht)? Are traditions important? Why (not)?
- Magst du Musikfeste? Warum (nicht)? Do you like music festivals? Why (not)?
- Was ist dein Lieblingsfest? Warum? What is your favourite festival? Why?
- Bist du zu einem Konzert gegangen? Have you been to a concert?

GRAMMAR

To meet

The verb 'to meet' can be translated in more than one way:

- treffen – to meet (up with someone) – e.g. Ich treffe meinen Freund im Restaurant.
- kennenlernen – to meet (to get to know) – e.g. Ich lerne gern neue Leute kennen.

WALES AND THE WORLD – AREAS OF INTEREST

HOME AND LOCALITY

The sub-theme of **Home and Locality** is divided into two areas. Here are some suggestions of topics to revise:

LOCAL AREAS OF INTEREST
- local facilities and amenities
- tourist attractions
- geographical features
- weather and climate
- advantages and disadvantages of where you live
- your local area in the past

TRAVEL AND TRANSPORT
- different types of transport
- advantages and disadvantages of types of transport
- different types of journey
- transport links
- buying tickets and booking a journey
- transport problems – e.g. delays, strikes, etc.

WRITING A FORMAL LETTER
1. Put your name and address top left and the name and address you are writing to top right, followed by the date underneath.
2. Use an appropriate opening greeting:
   Sehr geehrter Herr Braun – Dear Mr Braun
   Sehr geehrte Frau Schulz – Dear Mrs Schulz
   Sehr geehrte Damen und Herren – Dear Sir or Madam
3. Use Sie throughout the letter.
4. Use a formal ending to your letter – e.g. Mit freundlichen Grüßen.

WRITING AN INFORMAL LETTER/E-MAIL

There aren't any fixed rules when it comes to writing a letter or e-mail to a friend. You could start it off with:

   Liebe Julia – Dear Julia
   Lieber Stefan – Dear Stefan

Note the different endings depending on the gender of the person you are writing to.
   To sign off you could use:

   Bis bald – See you soon
   Tschüss – Bye
   Mit freundlichen Grüßen – Yours faithfully

LOCAL AREAS OF INTEREST

Wie findest du deine Gegend?
What do you think of your area?

Meine Stadt ist sehr dreckig. Es gibt viel Verschmutzung durch Autos und Industrie. Ich würde lieber an der Küste wohnen.
My town is very dirty. There is too much pollution due to cars and industry. I would prefer to live at the seaside.

Was gibt es für junge Leute in deiner Gegend?
What is there for young people in your area?

Es gibt nicht viel zu tun für junge Leute. Es gibt einige Geschäfte und ein Kino und das ist alles. Ich möchte ein Schwimmbad oder Tennisplätze haben.
There isn't much for young people to do. There are some shops and a cinema and that's it. I would like to have a swimming pool or tennis courts.

Was wirst du dieses Wochenende in deiner Gegend machen?
What are you going to do in your area this weekend?

Ich werde meine Freunde in der Stadtmitte treffen und wir werden ins Kino gehen. Leider hat meine Stadt nicht viele Attraktionen und ist ziemlich langweilig für junge Leute.
I'm going to meet my friends in the town centre and we will go to the cinema. Unfortunately, my town doesn't have many attractions and it's quite boring for young people.

Wie war deine Gegend in der Vergangenheit?
What was your area like in the past?

Vor Jahren war meine Stadt viel kleiner. Meine Großeltern haben mir erzählt, dass es viele Parks gab. Die Stadt war sehr ruhig. Heutzutage ist die Stadt sehr industriell und als Folge davon ist sie verschmutzt.
Years ago, my town was much smaller. My grandparents told me that there were lots of parks. The town was very quiet. Nowadays the town is very industrial and as a result it is polluted.

Wie würdest du deine Gegend verbessern?
How would you improve your area?

Ich würde viele Verbesserungen in meiner Stadt machen, wenn ich könnte, weil es am Wochenende nichts zu tun gibt. Meiner Meinung nach brauchen wir ein neues Einkaufszentrum.
I would make many improvements in my town, if I could, because there's nothing to do at the weekend. In my opinion, we need a new shopping centre.

It doesn't matter if you live in a huge, vibrant city or a tiny village miles from anywhere. You can make up details if you need to – no one is going to come round to check whether what you have said or written is true! As well as being able to describe your local area, you will need to offer opinions and discuss advantages and disadvantages.

GRAMMAR

Future plans

- You can just use **Ich möchte** plus an infinitive at the end of the sentence to say what you would like to do – e.g. **Ich möchte im Ausland wohnen.** I would like to live abroad.
- Or you can use the conditional tense to say what you would do – e.g. **Ich würde mehr Häuser bauen (, um meine Stadt zu verbessern).** I would build more houses (to improve my town).
- Use the correct form of **würden** plus an infinitive at the end of the sentence.
- When using the conditional with **haben** and **sein**, you will normally use **hätte** and **wäre**:

  Wenn ich reich **wäre**, würde ich ein modernes Haus kaufen. If I were rich, I would buy a new house.
  Wenn ich mehr Geld **hätte**, würde ich umziehen. If I had more money, I'd move.

EXAM TASK

Lies diese Werbungen.

A

Freizeitzentrum
Café und Bar
Vier Tennisplätze
Fußballfeld
Hallenbad
Turnhalle
Öffnungszeiten: 07h00–21h00 täglich

B

Stadtpark
Teestube
Kinderpark
Hunde erlaubt
Freier Eintritt
Freibad
Öffnungszeiten: 09h00–16h00 täglich
(außer Dienstag)

Wähle die Attraktion, wo man ...
1. jeden Tag besuchen kann.
2. schwimmen und trainieren kann.
3. ohne Geld besuchen kann.
4. im Freien schwimmen kann.
5. sechs Tage pro Woche besuchen kann.

Be careful with this common type of question. Distractors are harder to spot in German! Look for different words which have the same meaning – e.g. free = without money, every day = daily.

LOCAL AREAS OF INTEREST

USEFUL PHRASES

Ich wohne in einer großen Stadt in Wales.	I live in a big town in Wales.
Diese Gegend hat Vor- und Nachteile. Zum Beispiel ...	This area has advantages and disadvantages. For example …
Meine Stadt ist lebhaft mit hervorragenden öffentlichen Verkehrsmitteln.	My town is lively with excellent public transport.
Ich würde einen Besuch im Frühling empfehlen, weil das Wetter schön ist.	I would recommend a visit in spring because the weather is nice.
Meine Stadt ist berühmt für ihre Fußballmannschaft.	My town is famous for its football team.
Touristen könnten die Kathedrale und das Museum besuchen.	Tourists could visit the cathedral and the museum.
Meine Stadt hat sich sehr verbessert.	My town has improved a lot.
Viele Häuser werden gebaut.	Lots of houses are being built.
Wenn ich Bürgermeister/Bürgermeisterin wäre, würde ich die Reiseverbindungen verbessern.	If I were the mayor, I would improve the travel connections.
Wenn ich die Wahl hätte, würde ich auf dem Land wohnen.	If I had the choice, I would live in the countryside.
Um meine Gegend zu verbessern, würde ich mehr Attraktionen für Touristen bauen.	To improve my area, I would build more attractions for tourists.
Mein Bruder hätte gern einen Freizeitpark in der Nähe.	My brother would like a theme park nearby.
Ich glaube, dass es nicht genug für junge Leute gibt.	I think that there isn't enough for young people.
Samstagsabends gibt es Gewalt in der Stadtmitte und es gibt immer mehr Kriminalität.	On Saturday evenings there is violence in the town centre and there is more and more crime.
Die Kunstgalerie ist eine Reise wert.	The art gallery is worth a visit.

Some useful phrases for describing your area are:

es ist – it is
es war – it was
es gibt – there is/there are
es gab – there was/there were
es hat – it has
es hatte – it had

GRAMMAR

Perfect tense

You may need to talk about what you used to do in your area or what it was like. The perfect tense is used to talk about things which happened in the past. It is the most common way to talk about the past in German.

To form the perfect tense you need:

- The correct form of **haben** or **sein**.
- A past participle.

There are regular (e.g. **gespielt, gewohnt**) and irregular (e.g. **gegangen, gesehen**) past participles:

- Ich habe im Park **gespielt**.
- Er hat in der Stadtmitte **gewohnt**.

Remember that some verbs use **sein** instead of haben – e.g. Ich **bin** ins Kino gegangen.

EXAM TASK

Translate the following paragraph into German:

I like living in my village. There aren't many shops. My mum finds the area boring, because there's no sports centre. I'm going to live in Spain when I'm older.

Check carefully that you are using the correct tenses.

TRAVEL AND TRANSPORT

Wie fährst du gern? Warum?
How do you like to travel? Why?

Ich fliege am liebsten, weil es bequem und schnell ist. Mein Vater ist immer ganz nervös, wenn wir fliegen, aber ich finde es aufregend.
I prefer to fly as it's comfortable and quick. My father is always very nervous when we fly but I find it exciting.

Was sind die Vor- und Nachteile der öffentlichen Verkehrsmittel?
What are the advantages and disadvantages of public transport?

Öffentliche Verkehrsmittel sind gut für die Umwelt. Fünfzig Personen können in einem Bus fahren und das bedeutet weniger Autos auf den Straßen. Es ist praktisch und oft billiger.
Public transport is much more efficient. Fifty people can travel on a bus and that means fewer cars on the roads. It's practical and often cheaper.

Was sind die Nachteile, wenn man mit dem Auto fährt?
What are the disadvantages of travelling by car?

In meiner Stadt gibt es oft Staus. Es ist auch schwer einen Parkplatz zu finden und meine Mutter findet das sehr stressig. Trotzdem werde ich mit 17 Fahrstunden haben, obwohl sie teuer sind.
There are often traffic jams in my town. It's also difficult to find a parking space and my mother finds that very stressful. In spite of that I will have driving lessons when I'm 17, although they are expensive.

Wie bist du gestern zur Schule gekommen?
How did you get to school yesterday?

Normalerweise gehe ich zu Fuß, aber gestern hat es geregnet, also bin ich mit dem Auto gefahren.
Normally I go on foot but yesterday it was raining so I went by car.

Wie wirst du nächstes Jahr in den Urlaub fahren?
How will you travel for your holiday next year?

Nächsten Sommer werde ich mit meiner Familie nach Frankreich fahren und wir werden mit dem Auto und der Fähre fahren. Ich fahre gern mit der Fähre, weil es viel zu tun gibt. Meine Schwester ist normalerweise seekrank.
Next summer I will go to France with my family and we will travel by car and ferry. I like the ferry because there are lots of things to do. My sister is usually seasick.

GRAMMAR

Preferences

Gern, lieber, am liebsten are useful phrases when talking about what you like/prefer to do. They go after the verb:

- Ich fahre **gern** mit dem Rad. I like going by bike.
- Ich fahre **lieber** mit dem Auto. I prefer going by car.
- Ich fahre **am liebsten** mit dem Taxi. I like going by taxi most of all.

In questions they go after the pronoun:

- Fährst du **gern** mit dem Bus? Do you like travelling by bus?

Answer the questions in English.

EXAM TASK

Ist es möglich, von Hamburg nach Berlin für 14 Euro zu fahren? Mit dem Zug nicht, aber wenn Sie mit der Mitfahrzentrale[1] fahren, dann ist das ganz normal. Es gibt tausende von Fahrtangeboten[2] in Deutschland und Europa, die oft bis zu 75 Prozent billiger sind als mit dem Zug.

Das System ist natürlich besser für die Umwelt, ist einfach und es macht Spaß! Mit netten Mitfahrern ist die Reise nicht so langweilig. Man kann einen Platz auf der Webseite oder per SMS reservieren. Die meisten Fahrer sind pünktlich und freundlich. Falls[3] es Probleme gibt, sind wir jeden Tag 24 Stunden für Sie da!

1 car sharing agency
2 offers of journeys
3 in case of

1. What question is asked in the opening sentence?
2. Where is the service available?
3. What are you told about prices?
4. What other advantages are there? Write **two** details.
5. How can you make a booking?

TRAVEL AND TRANSPORT

Ich fahre mit dem Auto zur Schule, weil ich später das Haus verlassen kann.	I go to school by car because I can leave the house later.
Die Busfahrpläne in meinem Dorf sind unzuverlässig.	The bus timetables in my village are unreliable.
Wenn man mit dem Auto zur Schule oder Arbeit fährt, ist es umweltschädlich.	When you travel to school or work by car, it's harmful to the environment.
Wenn man in einer Großstadt wohnt, ist es oft schneller, mit den öffentlichen Verkehrsmittel zu fahren.	If you live in a big town, it's often quicker to use public transport.
Wenn man einen Sitzplatz im Zug finden kann, kann man lesen oder arbeiten.	If you can find a seat on the train, you can read or work.
Wenn man nicht weit von der Schule wohnt, sollte man zu Fuß gehen.	If you don't live too far from school, you should go there on foot.
Meiner Meinung nach ist Radfahren am umweltfreundlichsten.	In my opinion, cycling is the most environmentally friendly option.
Wenn man zu Fuß geht, ist es gut die Umwelt. Es ist auch gut für deine Gesundheit und natürlich kostenlos!	Walking is good for the environment. It's also good for your health and, of course, free!
Fahrstunden kosten viel Geld und die Autoversicherung ist oft unbezahlbar für junge Leute.	Driving lessons cost a lot of money and car insurance is often unaffordable for young people.
Zugfahrkarten sind oft sehr teuer, wenn man nicht im Voraus bucht.	Train tickets are often very expensive, if you don't book in advance.
Mit 18 werde ich ein Motorrad kaufen.	I will buy a motorbike when I'm 18.
Wenn man einen Führerschein hat, ist man viel unabhängiger.	When you have a driving licence, you're more independent.

This topic isn't just about buying a ticket! You need to be able to give opinions on different types of transport and make comparisons between them. Think of ways to include the past, present and future tenses in your answers.

In the speaking exam the first question on the photo card will ask you to describe the photo (or what is happening in it):

- Beschreibe das Foto./Was passiert auf diesem Foto?

The second question will usually ask you for an opinion – e.g.:

- Gibt es genug Fahrradwege in deiner Gegend? Warum (nicht)? Does your area have enough cycle lanes? Why (not)?

Your teacher will then ask you **two** unseen questions. In the first unseen question you will usually have to comment on an opinion – e.g.:

- Busse in der Gegend sind zu teuer. Was sagst du dazu? Local buses are too expensive. What do you think?

The last question will usually need to be answered in a different tense – e.g.:

- Wie bist du gestern zur Schule gekommen? How did you get to school yesterday?

In your preparation time, try to predict some of the things you might be asked in the unseen questions.

WALES AND THE WORLD – AREAS OF INTEREST

THE WIDER WORLD

The sub-theme of **The Wider World** is divided into two areas. Here are some suggestions of topics to revise:

LOCAL AND REGIONAL FEATURES AND CHARACTERISTICS OF GERMANY AND GERMAN-SPEAKING COUNTRIES

- places of interest in German-speaking countries
- geographical features
- weather and climate
- tourist attractions and monuments
- regional characteristics

HOLIDAYS AND TOURISM

- holiday locations and resorts
- types of holiday
- holiday accommodation
- holiday activities
- advantages and disadvantages of tourism
- different types of tourism
- problems and complaints

REMEMBER:

You will be marked for linguistic knowledge and accuracy in your speaking and writing exams. It is important to spend time revising basic things like:

- genders of nouns
- verb endings
- adjectives (and agreements)
- prepositions
- tenses

You are not expected to be an expert on every tourist attraction in Germany, but you should be able to talk generally about the topic.

LOCAL AND REGIONAL FEATURES AND CHARACTERISTICS OF GERMANY AND GERMAN-SPEAKING COUNTRIES

Warst du schon in Deutschland?
Have you ever been to Germany?

Ich habe Deutschland noch nie besucht, aber ich möchte Berlin besuchen, um die Sehenswürdigkeiten zu sehen. Ich finde Themenparks klasse, also würde ich gern nach Europa-Park in Südwestdeutschland gehen.
I've never visited Germany but I'd like to go to Berlin to see the sights. I love theme parks so I would like to go to Europa-Park in south-west Germany.

Besuchst du gern historische Gebäude? Warum (nicht)?
Do you like visiting historical buildings? Why (not)?

Ich weiß, dass Kultur und Geschichte wichtig sind, aber ehrlich gesagt finde ich Museen langweilig. Ich kaufe lieber Souvenirs.
I know that culture and history are important but to be honest I find museums boring. I prefer buying souvenirs.

Findest du deutsche Kultur interessant? Warum (nicht)?
Do you find German culture interesting? Why (not)?

Ich finde deutsche Kultur sehr interessant. Deutschland hat viele historische Gebäude und coole Traditionen. Ich möchte mehr darüber lernen.
I find German culture very interesting. Germany has lots of historical buildings and cool traditions. I'd like to learn more about them.

 If you've never been to Germany or a German-speaking country you can either make up a visit so you've got something to talk about or describe where you'd like to visit. There is a lot of overlap with the vocabulary you'll need for **local areas of interest**, just in a different context.

Welche Touristenattraktion hast du neulich besucht?
Which tourist attraction have you visited recently?

Letztes Wochenende haben wir die Kunstgalerie besucht. Es gab viele Touristen, aber es hat Spaß gemacht. Der Eintritt war kostenlos und das hat meiner Mutter gefallen.
Last weekend, we went to the art gallery. There were lots of tourists but it was fun. Entrance was free and that pleased my mother.

Wohin wirst du nächstes Jahr gehen?
Where will you go next year?

Ich werde nächsten Dezember mit der Schule in die Schweiz fahren, um Skiurlaub zu machen. Ich freue mich schon darauf, weil ich gern Zeit mit meinen Schulfreunden verbringe. Ich habe gehört, dass die Landschaft wunderschön ist.
Next December I will go to Switzerland with the school for a ski holiday. I'm looking forward to it because I enjoy spending time with my school friends. I've heard that the scenery is beautiful.

GRAMMAR

Prepositions

Prepositions give information about the position of a noun or pronoun. They change the case of the noun or pronoun. Prepositions often have more than one meaning – e.g.:

- mit dem Taxi – by taxi
- mit meinem Bruder – with my brother

Some prepositions are always followed by the accusative case – e.g. **für** (for), **um** (around/for/at), **durch** (through), **bis** (until), **ohne** (without), **wider** (against), **gegen** (against), **entlang** (along).

Some prepositions are always followed by the dative case – e.g. **bei** (at the house of), **aus** (from/out of), **nach** (to/after/past), **gegenüber** (opposite), **seit** (since/for), **von** (from), **außer** (except for), **mit** (with), **zu** (to).

Some prepositions are followed by the accusative or dative case depending on the meaning – e.g. **an** (on), **auf** (on), **hinter** (behind), **vor** (in front of/before), **in** (in), **unter** (under), **über** (over/above), **neben** (next to), **zwischen** (between).

- Ich gehe in die Stadt. I am going to town. (accusative – movement towards)
- Ich bin in der Stadt. I am in town. (dative – indicating position)

EXAM TASK

Translate the following paragraph into English:

Ich besuche gerne neue Länder, wenn ich in den Urlaub fahre. Letztes Jahr bin ich mit meiner Familie in die Schweiz gefahren. Meine Eltern interessieren sich für Geschichte, deswegen haben wir viele Museen und historische Gebäude besucht. Ich möchte nächstes Jahr nach Polen fahren, um mehr über die Kultur zu lernen.

Make sure you check that your English makes sense. Don't forget that the word order could be different in German.

LOCAL AND REGIONAL FEATURES AND CHARACTERISTICS OF GERMANY AND GERMAN-SPEAKING COUNTRIES

Du kannst neue Kulturen entdecken oder deine Fremdsprachenkenntnisse verbessern.

You can discover new cultures or improve your foreign language skills.

Wenn man sich für Geschichte interessiert, gibt es Museen und historische Monumente.

If you are interested in history, there are museums and historical monuments.

Touristen können interessante Sehenswürdigkeiten wie das Schloss besuchen.

Tourists can visit interesting sites like the castle.

Die Touristenattraktionen in Berlin sind weltberühmt.

The tourist attractions in Berlin are world-famous.

Die Stadt zieht jedes Jahr Millionen von Touristen an.

The town attracts millions of tourists every year.

Die Schweiz ist ein Traumziel für Wintersportler.

Switzerland is a dream destination for fans of winter sports.

Deutschland ist ein Traumziel für Touristen, die sich für Geschichte interessieren.

Germany is a dream destination for tourists who are interested in history.

Die Landschaft in Deutschland bietet mit Seen, Bergen und Küsten für jeden das Richtige.

The landscape of Germany, with lakes, mountains and coastlines, offers something for everyone.

Themenparks wie der Europa-Park und das Phantasialand werden immer beliebter.

Theme parks like Europa-Park and Phantasialand are becoming more and more popular.

Deutschland ist berühmt für das reiche kulturelle und literarische Erbe.

Germany is famous for its rich cultural and literary heritage.

Hamburg ist eine lebhafte Stadt, in der man viele Aktivitäten machen kann.

Hamburg is a lively town, in which you can do lots of activities.

Deutschland ist das zweitbeliebteste Reiseland Europas.

Germany is the second most popular tourist destination in Europe.

GRAMMAR

Imperatives

Commands are easy to form using Sie:

- Buchen Sie sofort. Book straight away.

Separable verbs:

- Rufen Sie uns an. Phone us.

To form commands using du, you use the du form of the present tense verb and take the -st off. You might also see this with an -e added in written German:

- Buch(e) sofort. Book straight away.
- Besuch(e) die Altstadt. Visit the old city.

Remember that some verbs are irregular in the du form:

- Nimm den Bus. Take the bus.
- Lies die Werbung. Read the advert.

EXAM TASK

Here are some examples of role play prompts on this topic.

Remember you don't need to give factual information. It's okay to make up answers.

- Say what the weather is like.
- Say what you normally do on holiday.
- Ask your friend a question about a tourist attraction.
- Ask your friend what they like to do on holiday.
- Say where you went last year.
- Say what tourist attraction you will visit next year.

You don't need to give extra information. For the first bullet point you could say something as simple as Es ist kalt to score full marks.

HOLIDAYS AND TOURISM

Was machst du normalerweise während der Sommerferien?
What do you normally do during the summer holidays?

Wir fahren normalerweise für eine Woche in den Urlaub. Wir bleiben auf einem Campingplatz in einem Wohnwagen. Meine Mutter surft das Internet, um ein Schnäppchen zu finden.
We go on holiday for a week every year. We stay on a campsite in a caravan. My mum uses the internet to find a bargain.

Was sind die positiven Aspekte des Tourismus?
What are the positive aspects of tourism?

Tourismus ist gut für die Wirtschaft. Er ist eine große Industrie, die viele Arbeitsplätze schafft.
Tourism is good for the economy. It's a big industry which creates many jobs.

Wohin fährst du lieber in Urlaub? Zum Strand oder in die Stadt? Warum?
What do you prefer? Holidays at the seaside or in town? Why?

Ich habe Strandurlaub am liebsten, weil ich gern Wassersport treibe. Ich bin gern aktiv und mache täglich verschiedene Aktivitäten, zum Beispiel Tauchen, Windsurfen und so weiter.
I prefer the beach because I like water sports. I like to be active and do different activities each day, for example, diving, windsurfing and so on.

Was hast du letztes Jahr gemacht?
What did you do last year?

Tagsüber sind wir zum Strand gegangen und ich habe mich gesonnt. Am letzten Tag sind wir in die Stadt gefahren und ich habe Souvenirs für meine Freunde gekauft. Der Urlaub war wunderbar!
During the day, we went to the beach and I sunbathed. On the last day, we went to town and I bought souvenirs for my friends. The holiday was great!

Was wäre dein Traumurlaub?
What would your dream holiday be like?

Mein Traumurlaub? Ich würde drei Wochen mit meiner Familie auf einer Insel in der Karibik verbringen. Es würde jeden Tag heiß und sonnig sein und wir würden in einem Luxushotel mit einem riesigen Schwimmbad mit Wasserrutschen wohnen.
My dream holiday? I would spend three weeks with my family on an island in the Caribbean. It would be hot and sunny every day and we would stay in a luxury hotel with a huge swimming pool with water slides.

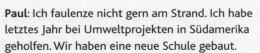

EXAM TASK

Lies die Texte und verbinde die Paare.

Katja: Am liebsten liege ich den ganzen Tag in der Sonne – Sand und Sonne sind perfekt für mich.

Paul: Ich faulenze nicht gern am Strand. Ich habe letztes Jahr bei Umweltprojekten in Südamerika geholfen. Wir haben eine neue Schule gebaut.

Sofia: Jedes Jahr fahren wir in die Schweiz. Mein Bruder und ich fahren gern Ski.

Markus: Campingplätze sind viel billiger als Luxushotels und ich bin gern in der frischen Luft.

Lotte: Letzten Dezember bin ich mit der Schule nach Frankreich gefahren. Die Reise war zu lang, aber das Hotel war klasse.

Florian: Wenn ich im Urlaub bin, gehe ich gern ins Museum. Kunstgalerien gefallen mir auch.

1. Zelturlaub
2. Klassenfahrt
3. Strandurlaub
4. Ökotourismus
5. Kulturtourismus
6. Wintersporturlaub

You should feel confident about using the past, present and future tenses in your spoken and written German.

You should be familiar with the following tenses:

- The present tense to talk about activities you do regularly – e.g. Ich fahre jedes Jahr nach Italien.
- The perfect tense to say what you have done – e.g. Ich habe das Stadion besucht. Ich bin nach Deutschland gefahren.
- The imperfect tense to talk about the past – e.g. Es war toll. Es gab nichts für Touristen. Ich hatte nicht genug Zeit.
- The future tense to say what you will do – e.g. Ich werde viel wandern.
- The conditional tense to say what you would do – e.g. Ich würde in einem Luxushotel wohnen (, wenn ich mehr Geld hätte).

Try to use a range of these tenses to improve your performance in your speaking and writing exams. You need to be able to recognise them as they will appear in your listening and reading exams.

HOLIDAYS AND TOURISM

Die Ruhe und frische Luft waren perfekt für uns.	The peace and fresh air were perfect for us.
Ich verbringe gern Zeit mit meiner Familie, obwohl wir manchmal uns streiten.	I like spending time with my family, although we sometimes argue.
Ich sonne mich gern am Strand.	I like sunbathing on the beach.
Normalerweise zelten wir, weil Hotels so teuer sind.	Usually we go camping because hotels are so expensive.
Als ich jünger war, habe ich gern Urlaub mit meinen Eltern gemacht, aber jetzt mache ich lieber Urlaub mit meinen Freunden.	When I was younger I liked holidaying with my parents but now I prefer spending my holidays with my friends.
Ich fahre lieber im Winter in den Urlaub, weil ich gern in den Bergen Ski fahre	I prefer going on holiday in winter because I like skiing in the mountains.
Es war eine unvergessliche Erfahrung.	It was an unforgettable experience.
Mein Urlaub war entspannend, weil das Hotel so bequem war.	My holiday was relaxing because the hotel was so comfortable.
Postkarten sind wegen Handys aus der Mode gekommen.	Postcards have gone out of fashion because of mobile phones.
Es gab keinen Internetzugang in unserem Ferienhaus und ich fand das ärgerlich.	There was no internet access in our holiday house and I found that annoying.
Als wir angekommen sind, sind wir sofort ins Schwimmbad gegangen.	When we arrived, we went to the swimming pool straight away.
Wir wollten zum Strand gehen, aber es hat geregnet.	We wanted to go to the beach but it rained.
Tourismus kann umweltfeindlich sein.	Tourism can be bad for the environment.
Es gibt manche Touristen, die keinen Respekt zeigen.	There are some tourists who don't show any respect.
Ich hoffe, schon bald hierher zurück zu kommen.	I hope to come back here soon.
Souvenirgeschäfte und Hotels zerstören die Landschaft.	The souvenir shops and hotels destroy the landscape.

GRAMMAR

Tenses

Are the following sentences in the present, past, future or conditional tense?

1. Ich habe das Museum besucht.
2. Es hat mir gut gefallen.
3. Ich werde das Stadion besuchen.
4. Was würdest du empfehlen?
5. Ich wohne in einem Dorf.
6. Es kostet zu viel.

EXAM TASK

Write a full sentence in German for each of the headings:

- transport
- accommodation
- weather
- meals
- activities
- your opinion

Make sure your sentence is complete and contains an appropriate verb – e.g. for the first bullet point you should say Ich fahre mit dem Auto not just mit dem Auto.

WALES AND THE WORLD – AREAS OF INTEREST

GLOBAL SUSTAINABILITY

The sub-theme of **Global Sustainability** is divided into two areas. Here are some suggestions of topics to revise:

ENVIRONMENT

- environmental issues
- recycling
- climate change
- drought and flooding
- pollution
- types of energy
- environmental groups

SOCIAL ISSUES

- charity events
- raising money
- worldwide problems – e.g. poverty, famine, health, homelessness
- volunteering

ADVICE

A task on the environment or social issues might seem harder than some of the other sub-themes. You will need to learn some topic-specific vocabulary but the expectations are the same as with all the other sub-themes. You need to express opinions and refer to events using the past, present and future tenses. Try to write extended sentences using connectives. You can combine more than one tense in a sentence and you can vary the vocabulary that you use to express opinions. When revising this sub-theme, it might be helpful to think of how you could do the following:

- express which social or environmental problems you are worried about and why
- talk about a charity you support and what it does
- talk about something that happened in the past – e.g. a charity event you attended
- say what you do at the moment to support charities or to help the environment
- talk about a future event – e.g. a cake sale you will organise, a fundraiser you will attend, your plans to volunteer, how you will become more eco-friendly, etc.
- say how young people can help or what people should do to help

ENVIRONMENT

Was sind die schlimmsten Umweltprobleme in deiner Gegend?
What are the worst environmental problems in your area?

Leider gibt es viele Probleme in meiner Gegend. Estens gibt es nicht genug Mülleimer und Leute werfen Müll auf den Boden. Ich glaube auch, dass es zu viele Autos auf den Straßen gibt. Als Folge gibt es ein großes Problem mit Luftverschmutzung.
Unfortunately, there are lots of problems in my area. Firstly, there aren't enough bins and people throw their rubbish on the floor. Also, I believe there are too many cars on the roads. As a result there's a big problem with air pollution.

Was sollte die Regierung machen, um der Umwelt zu helfen?
What should the government do to help the environment?

Ich glaube, dass die Regierung mehr machen könnte, um die Erde zu retten. Man muss mehr Geld in Solar- und Windenergie investieren. Man sollte auch Autos in der Innenstadt verbieten.
I think that the government could do more to save the Earth. More money needs to be invested in solar and wind energy. You should also ban cars in the city centre.

Findest du Recycling wichtig? Warum (nicht)?
Do you think recycling is important? Why (not)?

Ja. Natürlich ist Recycling sehr wichtig für unsere Umwelt und die Zukunft der Erde. Wenn wir recyceln, schonen wir die natürlichen Ressourcen.
Of course, recycling is very important for our environment and for the future of our planet. When we recycle, we save natural resources.

Was hast du neulich gemacht, um der Umwelt zu helfen?
What have you done recently to help the environment?

Heute Morgen habe ich mich geduscht, nicht gebadet, um Wasser zu sparen. Ich habe auch eine Stofftasche mitgenommen, um in den Supermarkt zu gehen.
This morning I had a shower instead of a bath to save water. Also I took a cloth bag to the supermarket.

Bist du umweltfreundlich? Warum (nicht)?
Are you environmentally friendly? Why (not)?

Ich mache so viel wie möglich, aber es ist manchmal schwer. Viele Produkte, die ich kaufe, enthalten Chemikalien. Ich werde in der Zukunft immer mehr Bioprodukte kaufen.
I do as much as possible but it's sometimes difficult. Many products which I buy contain chemicals. In the future, I will buy more organic products.

Wie könnte man Umweltprobleme in deiner Gegend verbessern?
How could you improve environmental problems in your area?

Meiner Meinung nach müssen wir Energie sparen. Zu Hause sollte man die Lichter ausmachen, wenn man das Zimmer verlässt, um Strom zu sparen. Das spart natürlich auch Geld.
In my opinion, we must save energy. At home, we should switch off lights when we leave a room to save electricity. That also saves money, of course.

The following are useful verbs for talking about the environment. Can you translate them into English? Can you write a sentence using each one? Vary your tenses where possible.

- helfen
- schützen
- reduzieren
- schaden
- sparen
- verschmutzen
- recyceln
- zerstören
- verursachen
- verschwenden
- benutzen

Quantifiers

Watch out for keywords which give more information or emphasise the meaning of numbers:

bis zu – up to
doppelt so viel – twice as much
fast – almost
im Durchschnitt – on average
knapp – barely/nearly
mehr als – more than
sinken – to sink/fall
steigen – to rise
weniger als – less than
zwischen – between

Answer the questions in English.
Heftige Unwetter in Bamberg, Süddeutschland
Gestern Abend sind zwischen 30 und 40 Liter Regen in einer Stunde gefallen. 2500 Menschen mussten ihre Häuser wegen des Hochwassers[1] verlassen und im Jugenzentrum übernachten. Es gibt weitere Warnungen für Überflutungen[2] in der Gegend, weil die Wettervorhersage für die nächsten drei Tage nicht gut aussieht. In Norddeutschland gab es Gewitter. In Hamburg gab es Berichte über Hagelkörner[3] so groß wie Golfbälle. Eiskalte Luft aus Grönland wird morgen Temperaturen von minus vier Grad bringen. Am Mittwoch wird es winterlich bleiben und am kommenden Wochenende wird es sehr windig und immer noch eiskalt sein.

1 high waters
2 flooding
3 hailstones

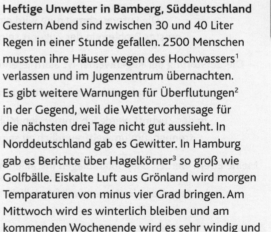

1. What was the weather like in Bamberg yesterday?
2. What happened as a result?
3. What warning is given?
4. What was unusual about the weather in Hamburg?
5. What is the forecast for the weekend?

ENVIRONMENT

Ich kaufe so oft wie möglich Fairtrade-Produkte.	I buy fair trade products as often as possible.
Ich nehme eine Stofftasche mit und fahre mit dem Bus, wenn ich in den Supermarkt gehe.	I take a reusable bag and use the bus when I go to the supermarket.
Man muss Energie sparen und erneuerbare Energie benutzen.	We must save energy and use renewable energy.
Meine Familie verschwendet zu viel Wasser.	My family wastes too much water.
Die Statistiken sind schockierend.	The statistics are shocking.
Der Treibhauseffekt erwärmt die Erde.	The greenhouse effect warms up the Earth.
Das Eis am Nord- und Südpol schmilzt.	The ice at the North and South Pole is melting.
Man sollte sich an das Tempolimit halten, weil das Benzin spart.	You should stick to the speed limit because that saves petrol.
Windräder produzieren viel Lärm und sehen schrecklich aus.	Wind turbines produce lots of noise and look awful.
Die Luftverschmutzung wird ein ernstes Problem in der Zukunft sein.	Air pollution will be a serious problem in the future.
Die Zerstörung der Regenwälder ist alarmierend.	The destruction of the rainforests is alarming.
Es gibt viele bedrohte Tierarten.	There are lots of endangered animals.
In der Zukunft werde ich immer den Müll trennen, um umweltfreundlich zu sein.	In the future I will always separate the rubbish to be environmentally friendly.
Meine Eltern werden bald Solaranlagen installieren.	My parents will soon install solar panels.
Leute werden immer umweltfreundlicher.	People are becoming more and more environmentally friendly.
Als ich jünger war, habe ich nichts gemacht, um die Erde zu retten.	When I was younger, I didn't do anything to save the Earth.

Write a sentence to describe an environmental problem using each of the following adjectives.

Remember to make them agree with the noun they are describing.

> weltweit – worldwide
> gefährlich – dangerous
> schädlich – harmful
> ernst – serious
> umweltfreundlich – environmentally friendly

EXAM TASK

Schreiben Sie einen Text für eine Internetseite über die Umwelt.

Sie können weitere Informationen geben, aber Sie müssen Informationen zu folgenden Themen schreiben:

- Umweltprobleme in deiner Gegend
- wie wichtig es ist, umweltfreundlich zu sein
- was du nächste Woche machen wirst, um der Umwelt zu helfen

Aim to write approximately 100 words. Try to stick within this limit. There are no extra marks for writing more than this! The second bullet point is asking for your opinions – try to justify them as much as possible. The third bullet point requires you to use the future tense.

SOCIAL ISSUES

Welches soziale Problem macht dir Sorgen?
Which social problem worries you?

Für mich ist es die Arbeitslosigkeit. Ich denke, dass die europäischen Regierungen mehr machen könnten, um die Situation zu verbessern.
For me, it's unemployment. I think that the European governments could do more to improve the situation.

Wie kann man das Problem der Armut lösen?
What can we do to solve the problem of poverty?

Leider gibt es keine einfache Lösung. Jeder sollte etwas Gutes für die Welt tun, zum Beispiel kann man Geld an Wohltätigkeitsorganisationen spenden.
Unfortunately, there isn't an easy solution. Everyone should do something good for the world, for example, you can give money to charities.

Gibt es ein Problem mit Obdachlosigkeit in deiner Gegend? Warum (nicht)?
Is there a problem with homelessness in your area? Why (not)?

Ich denke, dass das Problem der Obdachlosigkeit immer größer wird. Meiner Meinung nach sollte die Regierung mehr Häuser bauen und mehr Arbeitsplätze schaffen.
I think that the problem of homelessness is becoming bigger and bigger. In my opinion, the government should build more houses and create more jobs.

Was hast du neulich gemacht, um anderen Leuten zu helfen?
What have you done recently to help other people?

Ich habe Geld an Wohltätigkeitsorganisationen gespendet und ich habe einen Kuchenverkauf in der Schule organisiert.
I gave money to charities and I organised a cake sale at school.

Wie möchtest du anderen Leuten helfen?
What would you like to do to help other people?

Ich möchte mit armen Kindern arbeiten.
Nach meinen Prüfungen habe ich vor,
Freiwilligenarbeit zu leisten.
I would like to work with poor children. After
my exams, I intend to do voluntary work.

How to talk about social issues:

- Say which global issue worries you and use appropriate phrases to give your opinions – e.g. Das Problem, das mir Sorgen macht, ist … You could explain what kind of problems the issue causes or how it affects people. You could also say what you think will happen in the future.
- You need to give several reasons why it's important to help other people. You could also mention what you have done recently to help others – e.g. organising charity events at school, raising money, volunteering.
- You can mention what individuals can do – e.g. Man kann … , or should do – e.g. Man sollte … , and what the government should do – e.g. Die Regierung muss … You can also use Man könnte … to say what individuals could do. You could use other conditional verbs – e.g. Ich würde … and a range of connectives – e.g. wenn, dass, obwohl, damit.

EXAM TASK

Answer the questions in English.

Peter: Es ist vielleicht nicht sehr originell, aber meiner Meinung nach sollten wir Kuchen backen. Es ist sehr einfach und alle Studenten würden etwas in der Pause kaufen. Ich backe gern und habe einige gute Rezepte. Wenn man keine Zeit zum Backen hat, könnte man etwas im Supermarkt oder in der Bäckerei kaufen.

Krzystof: Ich glaube, dass ein Flohmarkt in der Schule eine gute Idee wäre. Wir haben bestimmt alle Weihnachts- oder Geburtstagsgeschenke, die wir nicht wollen. Jede Familie hat alte Spielzeuge im Keller. Wir könnten diese Dinge holen und dann verkaufen.

1. What does Peter say about his idea to bake cakes? Write **two** details.
2. What can you do if you don't have time to bake?
3. What does Krzystof plan on selling at the flea market? Write **three** details.

Read the text once, then read the questions, then read the text again. Use cognates (words that are similar to English ones) or near cognates to help you work out the meaning of certain words.

SOCIAL ISSUES

Heutzutage ist die Arbeitslosigkeit ein großes Problem.	These days, unemployment is a big problem.
Viele Menschen müssen im Freien schlafen – in Parks oder unter Brücken.	Many people have to sleep outside – in parks or under bridges.
Unsere Regierung sollte Entwicklungsländern helfen.	Our government should help developing countries.
Tausende Menschen weltweit haben nicht genug zu essen.	Thousands of people worldwide don't have enough to eat.
Gesundheitsorganisationen warnen, dass das Problem schlimmer werden wird.	Health organisations warn that the problem will get worse.
Es ist nötig, die Menschenrechte zu schützen.	It's necessary to protect human rights.
Die Obdachlosen haben oft zahlreiche Probleme wie Hunger, Arbeitslosigkeit und Alkoholismus.	Homeless people often have numerous problems such as hunger, unemployment and alcoholism.
Wir müssen gegen Rassismus kämpfen.	We must fight against racism.
Es ist ein internationales Problem.	It's an international problem.
Tatsächlich bedroht dieses Problem unsere Gesellschaft.	In fact, this problem threatens our society.
In den Großstädten gibt es nicht genug Häuser und Arbeitsplätze.	There aren't enough houses or jobs in the big cities.
Viele Leute sind Opfer der Wirtschaftskrise.	Many people are victims of the economic crisis.
Alle Länder müssen zusammenarbeiten, um das Problem zu lösen.	All countries must work together to solve the problem.

Top tips for the conversation:

- Listen carefully to the question. Work out whether the question uses the present, past or future tense so that you can use the same tense in your answer.
- Speak clearly and loudly.
- Don't worry if you hesitate. Don't use 'umm' or 'err' as we do in English but try to use some German phrases instead, for example Moment mal or Lass mich denken.
- Give a reason or an opinion wherever possible – don't just answer yes or no – ja oder nein. Learn three different ways of expressing 'I think that' or 'in my opinion' in German and try to use these phrases in your answers.
- Say lots! The conversation is your chance to show what you can do.

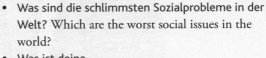

EXAM TASK

Here are some possible questions to which you can prepare answers. Practise them aloud and work on your accent.

- Was sind die schlimmsten Sozialprobleme in der Welt? Which are the worst social issues in the world?
- Was ist deine Lieblingswohltätigkeitsorganistion? Warum? Which is your favourite charity? Why?
- Wie kann man benachteiligten Kindern helfen? How can you help underprivileged children?
- Was hast du in der Schule gemacht, um anderen Leuten zu helfen? What have you done at school to help other people?
- Was machst du, um Wohltätigkeitsorganisationen zu helfen? What do you do to help charities?
- Was wirst du in der Zukunft machen, um Wohltätigkeitsorganisationen zu helfen? What will you do in the future to help charities?

CURRENT AND FUTURE STUDY AND EMPLOYMENT

CURRENT STUDY

The sub-theme of **Current Study** is divided into two areas. Here are some suggestions of topics to revise:

SCHOOL/COLLEGE LIFE

- school day
- comparison of the school system in different countries
- school facilities
- school trips
- clubs
- rules and regulations
- advantages and disadvantages of school uniform

SCHOOL/COLLEGE STUDIES

- subjects and opinions
- examinations
- workload
- advantages and disadvantages of homework
- study problems
- the importance of education

SCHOOL/COLLEGE LIFE

Wie findest du deine Schuluniform?
What do you think of your school uniform?

Ich denke, dass meine Schuluniform praktisch und ziemlich bequem ist. Es ist eine gute Idee, weil alle Schüler gleich aussehen. Es gibt keinen Unterschied zwischen armen und reichen Schülern. Andererseits verliert man die Individualität.
I think that my school uniform is practical and quite comfortable. It's a good idea because all students look the same. There's no difference between poor and rich students. On the other hand, individuality is lost.

Was für Aktivitäten machst du nach der Schule?
What after-school activities do you do?

Im Moment mache ich gar nichts, weil ich zu viele Hausaufgaben bekomme, aber letztes Jahr bin ich zum Informatikclub gegangen. Nach meinen Prüfungen möchte ich mehr Aktivitäten machen.
At the moment, I don't do anything because I get too much homework but last year I went to computer club. After my exams, I'd like to do more activities.

Wie findest du die Lehrer in deiner Schule?
What are the teachers like in your school?

Wir haben Glück, weil unsere Lehrer sehr geduldig sind und uns immer helfen. Jedoch ist meine Chemielehrerin zu streng.
We are lucky because our teachers are very patient and always help us. However, my chemistry teacher is too strict.

Was hast du gestern in der Schule gemacht?
What did you do in school yesterday?

Gestern hatte ich zwei Prüfungen, deswegen war ich gestresst. Ich hoffe, dass ich gute Noten bekommen werde!
Yesterday I had two exams, so I was stressed. I hope that I will get good marks!

Wie wäre deine Traumschule?
What would your ideal school be like?

Meine ideale Schule würde einen großen Sportplatz haben, weil ich sehr sportlich bin. Wir würden auch keine Schuluniform tragen. Der Schultag würde später beginnen, damit ich länger im Bett bleiben könnte.
My ideal school would have a large sports ground, because I'm very sporty. We wouldn't have to wear school uniform. The school day would begin later so I could stay in bed longer.

GRAMMAR

Imperfect tense

In more formal writing, the imperfect tense is usually used to talk about events in the past. There are a few examples in the extract below from a literary text:

- Ich fühlte – I felt
- Ich saß – I sat

It is useful to be familiar with verbs which are commonly used in the imperfect tense:

- Ich hatte – I had
- Ich war – I was

It is also useful to be able to recognise other forms of the imperfect tense, especially in literary texts.

EXAM TASK

Answer the questions about this literary text in English.

Jetzt muss ich wohl erst mal was über mich erzählen. Ich heiße Martin. Eigentlich bin ich ein ganz normaler Junge. Ein bisschen dick vielleicht. Ich trage auch eine Brille. Sie hat zentimeterdicke, viereckige Gläser. Ich hoffe, dass das Ding im Sportunterricht kaputtgeht. Das ist auch der einzige Grund, warum ich überhaupt beim Sport mitmache. Dann bekomme ich eine neue Brille oder Kontaktlinsen.

Ich fühlte mich an diesem ersten Schultag total nervös. Ich saß in der großen Aula mit meiner Mutter.

Und dann ...

„Ebermann, Martin", hat der Direktor gesagt.

„Klasse Fünf c."

Ich merkte, wie ich rot wurde. Ich hatte das Gefühl, alle glotzen mich an und lachen.

1. How does Martin describe himself? Write **two** details.
2. What's the only reason he takes part in PE lessons?
3. How does he feel on his first day at school?
4. What is he waiting for in the hall?
5. How does he feel when his name is called out?

Questions on literary texts may be longer and require more thought than the questions at the start of your reading paper, so make sure you leave enough time to answer them.

SCHOOL/COLLEGE LIFE

Die Schulgebäude sind ziemlich alt, aber glücklicherweise haben wir moderne Computereinrichtungen.

The buildings in my school are quite old but luckily we have modern computer facilities.

Ich finde die Schulregeln ziemlich streng, aber im Allgemeinen sind sie fair.

My school rules are quite strict but they are generally fair.

Ich denke, dass meine Schule zu streng ist, weil Handys verboten sind.

I think my school is too strict because mobile phones are not allowed.

Die Gründe für Mobbing sind vielfältig.

The reasons for bullying are numerous.

Leider gibt es Mobbing in jeder Schule.

Unfortunately there is bullying in every school.

Es ist wirklich schwer, dieses Problem zu lösen, aber Eltern, Schüler und Lehrer müssen zusammenarbeiten.

It's really difficult to solve this problem but parents, pupils and teachers must work together.

Ich bin unter Druck, weil ich viele Prüfungen habe.

I'm under pressure, because I have lots of exams.

Schwänzen ist ein großes Problem in meiner Schule.

Truancy is a big problem in my school.

Nach meiner Ansicht ist der Schultag zu lang.

In my opinion the school day is too long.

Ich bin gegen Schuluniformen, weil sie nicht modisch sind. Im Sommer ist die Jacke viel zu heiß.

I'm against school uniforms because they're not fashionable. The jacket is much too hot in summer.

In der Pause treffe ich meine Freunde und ich esse Süßigkeiten.

During breaktime, I meet my friends and eat sweets.

In der Mittagspause esse ich in der Kantine. Es gibt eine gute Auswahl und das Essen ist ziemlich gesund – zum Beispiel keine Pommes!

During the lunch break, I eat in the canteen. There is a lot of choice and the meals are quite healthy – for example, no chips!

You may be asked to describe your school day in your speaking or writing exam. Look at this description:

Die Schule beginnt um neun Uhr und endet um drei Uhr. Es gibt fünf Stunden pro Tag und jede Stunde dauert fünfzig Minuten. Die Pause ist um elf Uhr und Mittagessen ist um halb eins.

Try not to give answers like this all the time. This is correct German but it's just a list! There are no opinions, no justifications, no reasons and it's all in one tense. This would be a much better answer:

Die Schule beginnt um neun Uhr und endet um drei Uhr. Meiner Meinung nach ist der Schultag zu lang. Es gibt fünf Stunden pro Tag und jede Stunde dauert fünfzig Minuten. Gestern hatte ich eine Dopplestunde Mathe. Ich habe das langweilig gefunden. Die Pause ist um elf Uhr. Normalerweise spiele ich Fußball auf dem Schulhof.

Remember:

In your role play you will have to use the present tense as well as at least one other tense. Watch out for 'trigger' words which show you which tense to use – e.g. yesterday and last weekend show you need to use the past tense, and tomorrow and next week show you need to use the future tense.

If there are no trigger words – as in the first two bullet points that follow – then you will need to use the present tense.

- Describe your school.
- Give your opinion of school uniform.
- Say what you did at break time yesterday.
- Say what homework you did last week.
- Say what you will do tomorrow after school.
- Say what subjects you will study next week.

EXAM TASK

SCHOOL/COLLEGE STUDIES

Was ist dein Lieblingsfach? Warum?
What is your favourite subject? Why?

Im Augenblick ist mein Lieblingsfach Geschichte, weil die Arbeit faszinierend ist und der Lehrer lustig ist. Meine Freunde sind auch in dieser Klasse und zum Glück bekommen wir selten Hausaufgaben.
My favourite subject at the moment is history as the work is fascinating and the teacher is funny. My friends are also in this class and luckily we rarely get homework.

Findest du Prüfungen wichtig?
Do you think exams are important?

Die Prüfungen sind total wichtig, wenn man erfolgreich sein will. Ich werde Nachhilfe für Mathe bekommen, weil meine Noten nicht gut genug sind.
Exams are essential if you want to be successful. I will have private tuition in maths because my grades aren't good enough.

Ist das Schulleben stressig?
Is school life stressful?

Ja. Meine Eltern und Lehrer setzen mich unter Druck. Alles ist stressig! Man muss immer härter arbeiten, um erfolgreich zu sein. Wir bekommen täglich Hausaufgaben und ich habe keine Freizeit.
Yes. My parents and my teachers put me under pressure. Everything is stressful! You have to work harder and harder to be successful. We get homework every day and I don't have any free time.

Was hast du letztes Wochenende gemacht?
What did you do last weekend?

Ich wollte ins Kino gehen, aber ich hatte keine Zeit. Ich musste das ganze Wochenende Schularbeit machen. Es war anstrengend und langweilig.
I wanted to go to the cinema but I didn't have time. I had to do schoolwork all weekend. It was tiring and boring.

Was wirst du nächstes Jahr lernen?
What are you going to study next year?

Ich habe immer gute Noten in Naturwissenschaften bekommen und ich mache gern Experimente. Ich werde Biologie weiterlernen, aber ich muss noch zwischen Chemie und Physik wählen. Ich werde Erdkunde abwählen, weil es mich überhaupt nicht interessiert.
I've always had good grades in science and I like doing experiments. I am going to continue with biology but I still need to choose between chemistry and physics. I'm going to drop geography because it doesn't interest me at all.

You are likely to have at least one multiple-choice question in your reading and/or listening exam.
The question may be in English or German or use pictures. Top tips:

- Don't answer too soon! Make sure you read **all** of the options before choosing your answer and don't just stop when you come to the one that seems most likely.
- Some of the answers may be deliberately trying to trick you! Several alternatives may seem correct, so it is important to read the text and the questions carefully.
- If you are not sure of an answer, guess … but do so methodically. Eliminate some choices you know are wrong. Try to narrow down the answer to one or two alternatives and then compare them. Finally, make an informed decision.

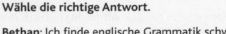

EXAM TASK

Now practise your multiple-choice strategies on this task.
Wähle die richtige Antwort.

Bethan: Ich finde englische Grammatik schwer zu verstehen. Ich würde lieber Spanisch lernen, weil es einfacher ist.

Paul: Chemie finde ich schwer. Ich möchte nächstes Jahr Biologie studieren, weil ich in der Zukunft als Tierarzt arbeiten will.

Emine: Ich mache viermal pro Woche Sport, deswegen habe ich keine Lust, Sport auch in der Schule zu studieren. Ich würde lieber etwas Kreatives studieren.

Florian: Ich habe keine Zeit, viele Bücher zu lesen. Ich hätte gern keine Deutschstunden!

1. Bethan möchte … lernen.
   a. Englisch
   b. eine neue Fremdsprache
   c. Grammatik
2. Paul will mit … arbeiten.
   a. Tieren
   b. Kindern
   c. Computern
3. Emine möchte … studieren.
   a. Sport
   b. Mathe
   c. Kunst
4. Florian braucht …
   a. neue Bücher.
   b. mehr Zeit.
   c. Hilfe.

SCHOOL/COLLEGE STUDIES

Ich bin gut in der Schule und ich gebe immer mein Bestes.	I'm good at school and I always do my best.
Der Lehrer erklärt alles gut und ich finde die Stunden motivierend.	The teacher explains well and the lessons are always motivating.
Ich langweile mich in der Stunde und der Lehrer gibt uns immer viele Hausaufgaben.	I get bored in the lesson and the teacher always gives us lots of homework.
Die Stunden sind nie interessant.	The lessons are never interesting.
Dieses Fach wird in der Zukunft (nicht) nützlich sein.	This subject will (not) be useful in the future.
Ich bin stark in Musik und ich spiele im Orchester.	I'm good at music and I play in the orchestra.
Ich bin schwach in Kunst und bekomme immer schlechte Noten.	I'm not good at art and always get bad marks.
Ich habe immer gern Mathe gelernt, weil ich gern rechne.	I've always loved maths, because I like doing sums.
Manche Fächer sind wichtig, um einen guten Beruf zu finden, zum Beispiel Fremdsprachen.	Some subjects are essential for finding a good job, for example, languages.
Ich kann mich in der Klasse nicht konzentrieren.	I can't concentrate in class.
Ich bin immer nervös, wenn ich eine Prüfung habe.	I'm always nervous when I have an exam.
Wenn ich gestresst bin, kann ich nicht schlafen.	When I'm stressed, I can't sleep.
Ich glaube, dass Deutsch wichtiger als Französisch ist.	I believe that German is more important than French.
Ich würde gern eine neue Fremdsprache lernen.	I would like to learn a new language.
Letztes Jahr war mein Englischlehrer streng und nervig.	Last year my English teacher was strict and annoying.
In der Grundschule waren meine Lehrer sehr hilfsbereit. Die Stunden haben Spaß gemacht.	At primary school, my teachers were very helpful. The lessons were fun.
Ich habe früher Chemie gelernt, aber es war zu schwierig.	Before, I used to study chemistry but it was too difficult.

Remember that you will be marked for accuracy at both Foundation and Higher level. Carefully check spellings, accents, genders, plurals and tenses.

Remember to include additional tenses, if possible, to show off your grammatical knowledge. In this task, for example, you are asked to write about your primary school (past tense) and your plans for September (future tense). Then, why not try to talk about your ideal school or what you would like to do in the future as well (conditional tense)?

As with the conversation part of the speaking exam, this is your opportunity to show what you can do. If you're not quite sure how to say something, write it another way – it doesn't have to be true as long as it makes sense!

You are in control in the writing exam but don't just write what you want for this task – make sure you answer the question and spend equal time on all three bullet points!

EXAM TASK

Schreibe einen Artikel für die Schulwebseite. Gib Information und Meinungen zu folgenden Themen:
- wie deine Grundschule war
- wie deine Schule ist
- welche Fächer du nächstes Jahr lernen wirst

CURRENT AND FUTURE STUDY AND EMPLOYMENT

ENTERPRISE, EMPLOYABILITY AND FUTURE PLANS

The sub-theme of **Enterprise, Employability and Future Plans** is divided into four areas. Here are some suggestions of topics to revise:

EMPLOYMENT
- advantages and disadvantages of employment and work experience
- saving money
- pocket money
- voluntary work
- part-time jobs
- how you spend the money you earn

SKILLS AND PERSONAL QUALITIES
- personality traits
- personal skills
- skills for different jobs
- application letters
- job interviews

POST-16 STUDY
- job and college applications
- formal letters
- CVs
- interviews – e.g. for work, college and university
- job and course adverts

CAREER PLANS
- training and study options
- job opportunities
- working abroad
- future plans
- interviews at an employment agency

EMPLOYMENT

Was machst du, um Geld zu verdienen?
What do you do to earn money?

Früher habe ich in einem Geschäft gearbeitet und ich habe viel Geld verdient, aber jetzt habe ich zu viel Schularbeit. Ich habe Glück, weil ich jede Woche Taschengeld von meinen Eltern bekomme, wenn ich im Haushalt helfe.
Before, I used to work in a shop and I earned a lot of money but now I have too much schoolwork. I am lucky because my parents give me pocket money every week if I help at home.

Ist es wichtig, in den Schulferien zu arbeiten?
Is it important to work in the school holidays?

Im Allgemeinen glaube ich, dass es eine gute Idee ist, wenn junge Leute in den Schulferien arbeiten. Man hat die Möglichkeit, etwas Neues zu lernen und Geld zu verdienen.
In general, I think it's a good idea for young people to work in the school holidays. It gives them the opportunity to learn new things and earn money.

Was sind die Nachteile von einem Teilzeitjob?
What are the disadvantages of having a part-time job?

Meine Freunde sagen, dass ihre Jobs schlecht bezahlt sind. Die Arbeit kann eintönig sein und man kann weniger Zeit für Hausaufgaben haben.
My friends tell me that their jobs are badly paid. The work can be monotonous and you can have less time for homework.

Möchtest du einen Sommerjob?
Would you like a holiday job?

Ich möchte im Freien als Schwimmlehrer(in) arbeiten. Ich würde gern mit Kindern arbeiten.
I would like to work outdoors as a swimming instructor. I would like to work with children.

> **Hast du Arbeitspraktikum gemacht?**
> Have you done work experience?

> **Nein, ich habe kein Arbeitspraktikum gemacht. In der Zukunft möchte ich als Journalist(in) arbeiten. Ich hätte gern Erfahrungen bei einer Zeitung gemacht.**
> No, I have never done work experience. In the future, I would like to be a journalist. I would have liked to have gained experience at a newspaper.

There are three ways of saying you in German:
1. Du is the informal version if you are talking to one person.
   Wo arbeitest du? Where do you work?
2. Ihr is the informal version if you are talking to two or more people.
   Wo arbeitet ihr? Where do you work?
3. Sie is the formal version.
   Wo arbeiten Sie? Where do you work?

Du or Sie?

Rewrite the questions using the Sie form (formal) instead of the du form (informal).

1. Machst du gern Prüfungen?
2. Arbeitest du gern mit Kindern?
3. Wo möchtest du studieren?
4. Bekommst du Taschengeld?
5. Bist du kreativ?
6. Hast du genug Geld?

Answer the questions in English.

Mein Name ist Angela. Ich werde nächsten Monat ein Arbeitspraktikum in einer Grundschule machen. Ich freue mich darauf, obwohl ich auch ein bisschen nervös bin. Das wäre gut für meinen Lebenslauf. Ich arbeite gern mit Kindern und in der Zukunft möchte ich als Sportlehrerin in einer Gesamtschule arbeiten. Ich werde auch gute Qualifikationen brauchen, aber ich möchte so viel Berufserfahrung wie möglich bekommen. In meiner Gegend ist es schwer, einen Job zu finden. Es gibt eine hohe Arbeitslosigkeit, besonders unter Jugendlichen. Ich muss morgen die Schule telefonieren, um Details über den Arbeitstag und so weiter herauszufinden. Ich werde auch fragen, was ich tragen soll.

1. What is Angela doing next month?
2. Why is she looking forward to it? Write **two** details.
3. What problem is there in her area?
4. What does she need to find out? Write **two** details.

EMPLOYMENT

Es ist wichtig, Erfahrung in der Arbeitswelt zu bekommen.	It's important to get experience in the world of work.
Ich habe den ganzen Tag an der Kasse gearbeitet.	I worked all day on the till.
Man muss hart in der Schule arbeiten, um die Prüfungen zu bestehen. Ich habe keine Zeit für einen Teilzeitjob.	You have to work hard at school to pass exams. I have no time for a part-time job.
Mein Arbeitspraktikum hat mir gut gefallen.	I really enjoyed my work experience.
Ich habe mich gut mit meinem Manager verstanden, obwohl er manchmal ungeduldig war.	I got on well with my boss, although he was sometimes impatient.
Früher haben alle Schüler ein Arbeitspraktikum gemacht, aber jetzt ist es nicht möglich in meiner Schule.	Before, all pupils used to do work experience, but now it's not possible in my school.
Ich möchte meine Fremdsprachenkenntnisse in meinem zukünftigen Beruf benutzen.	I'd like to use my foreign language skills in my future career.
Ich lerne neue Leute bei der Arbeit kennen und ich langweile mich nie.	I meet new people at work and I never get bored.
Der Arbeitstag hat früh begonnen und die Pausen waren zu kurz.	The working day started early and the breaks were too short.
Ich spare Geld, wenn ich kann.	I save money, when I can.
Sie können dann entscheiden, ob sie das Geld ausgeben oder sparen möchten.	They can then decide if they would like to spend or save the money.
Ich gebe mein Taschengeld sofort aus und ich spare nie.	I spend my pocket money straight away and I never save.
Kinder und Jugendliche können durch Taschengeld lernen, wie man mit seinem Geld umgeht.	Children and young people can learn how to deal with money through getting pocket money.
Sie bekommen mehr Verantwortung und werden unabhängiger.	They have more responsibility and become more independent.
Wenn ich mehr Zeit hätte, würde ich eine Teilzeitjob finden.	If I had more time, I'd find a part-time job.

Expressing opinions:

Meiner Meinung nach/Nach meiner Ansicht – In my opinion
Ich denke, dass … – I think that …
Ich glaube, dass … – I believe that …
Ich finde, dass … – I find that …
Es scheint mir, dass … – It seems to me that …
Man sagt, dass … – They say that …
Ich weiß, dass … – I know that …
Was ich am liebsten/wenigsten mag, ist … – What I like the most/least is …

AM TASK

Answer the questions in German.

- Beschreibe das Foto./Was passiert auf diesem Foto? Describe the photo./ What is happening in the photo?
- Ist es wichtig, viel Geld zu verdienen? Warum (nicht)? Is it important to earn a lot of money? Why (not)?
- Junge Leute brauchen Erfahrungen in der Arbeitswelt. Was sagst du dazu? Young people need experience of the world of work. What do you think?
- Möchtest du einen Teilzeitjob? Warum (nicht)? Would you like a part-time job? Why (not)?

Useful phrases for describing a picture:

auf diesem Foto – in the photo
ich sehe – I see
es gibt – there is
man kann … sehen – one can see
es zeigt – it shows
im Hintergrund – in the background
im Vordergrund – in the foreground

SKILLS AND PERSONAL QUALITIES

Welche persönlichen Qualitäten hast du?
What are your personal qualities?

Meine Lehrer würden sagen, dass ich immer freundlich und fleißig bin. Ich kann sowohl mit Kindern als auch mit Erwachsenen reden.
My teachers would say that I'm always friendly and hard-working. I can talk with both children and adults.

Welche Fähigkeiten hast du für die Arbeitswelt?
What are your skills for the world of work?

Meiner Meinung nach arbeite ich gut in einem Team, weil ich mit anderen Leuten gut auskomme. Ich habe auch gute Kommunikationsfähigkeiten.
In my opinion, I work well in a team because I get on well with other people. I also have good communication skills.

Welche Fähigkeiten suchen Arbeitgeber?
What skills do employers look for?

Wenn man einen guten Beruf finden will, muss man wenigstens eine Fremdsprache sprechen. Um erfolgreich zu sein, muss man risikobereit sein.
If you want to find a good job, it's best to speak at least one foreign language. To be successful, you have to be prepared to take risks.

Arbeitest du lieber alleine oder in einer Gruppe?
Do you prefer to work alone or in a group?

Ich arbeite lieber alleine, weil ich unabhängig bin. Es nervt mich, wenn mir andere Leute nicht zuhören. In einer Gruppe gibt es zu viel Streit.
I prefer to work alone, because I'm independent. It annoys me when other people don't listen to me. There are too many arguments in a group.

Welche Fähigkeiten möchtest du in der Zukunft lernen?
Which skills would you like to learn in the future?

Ich möchte meine Fremdsprachenkenntnisse verbessern und würde gerne im Ausland wohnen. Ich werde nächstes Jahr Fahrstunden nehmen, weil es nützlich ist, einen Führerschein zu haben.
I'd like to improve my foreign language skills and would like to live abroad. I will take driving lessons next year, because it's useful to have a driving licence.

When you are talking about your skills and personal qualities you will often need to give examples to illustrate the points you are making.
Here are some useful expressions in German:

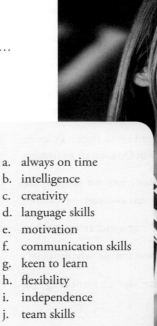

> **zum Beispiel** – for example
> **wie** – like/as
> **beispielweise** – by way of example
> **laut** – according to
> **entweder … oder …** – either … or …
> **als Beispiel nehmen wir …** – as an example let's take …
> **es ist klar, dass** – it is obvious that
> **darüber hinaus** – furthermore

EXAM TASK

Match 1–10 to a–j.

1. Kreativität
2. Teamfähigkeit
3. Sprachkenntnisse
4. Selbständigkeit
5. Intelligenz
6. Flexibilität
7. Lernbereitschaft – Man lernt gern neue Dinge
8. Pünktlichkeit
9. Kommunikationsfähigkeit
10. Motivation

a. always on time
b. intelligence
c. creativity
d. language skills
e. motivation
f. communication skills
g. keen to learn
h. flexibility
i. independence
j. team skills

SKILLS AND PERSONAL QUALITIES

Ich passe mich leicht an neue Situationen an.	I adapt easily to new situations.
Ich habe ausgezeichnete Kommunikationsfähigkeiten.	I have excellent communication skills.
Ich bin immer bereit, etwas Neues zu lernen.	I'm always ready to learn something new.
Man kann nützliche Kontakte finden.	You can find useful contacts.
Ich bin sehr praktisch und arbeite gern mit meinen Händen.	I am very practical and like working with my hands.
Ich muss meine Computerkenntnisse verbessern.	I need to improve my computer skills.
Ich möchte meine Sprachkenntnisse verbessern.	I would like to improve my language skills.
Ich kann zwischen den Zeilen lesen und Probleme lösen.	I can read between the lines and solve problems.
Ick kann Kritik akzeptieren, wenn sie konstruktiv ist.	I can accept criticism, when it's constructive.
Ich strebe danach, alle meine Ziele zu erreichen.	I strive to achieve all my goals.
Ich habe mir für die Zukunft anspruchsvolle Ziele gesetzt.	I have set myself ambitious goals for the future.
Die meisten Leute finden es leicht, ihre positiven Qualitäten zu nennen.	Most people find it easy to name their positive qualities.
Man muss gut zuhören und Ideen von anderen akzeptieren.	You need to listen well and accept the ideas of others.
Ich kann mehrere Dinge gleichzeitig machen.	I can multitask.
Ich war schon immer sehr motiviert.	I have always been very motivated.
Als ich jünger war, war ich nicht ehrgeizig.	When I was younger, I wasn't ambitious.

You will need to use appropriate vocabulary to emphasise the points you are making.

Here are some useful expressions in German:

vor allem – above all

besonders – especially

insbesondere – particularly

nämlich – specifically/namely

selbst wenn – even if

wobei – whereas

tatsächlich – in fact

außerdem – furthermore

EXAM TASK

Write one full sentence in German for each job:

- doctor
- teacher
- pilot
- police officer
- secretary
- IT technician

Look at the exam task on page 95. Try to use some of the vocabulary to help you here.

POST-16 STUDY

Möchtest du nächstes Jahr in der Schule weiterlernen?
Do you want to continue your studies next year?

Meiner Meinung nach ist das Schulleben stressig, aber ich will in der Zukunft einen guten Beruf haben, deswegen werde ich weiterlernen. Ich werde Englisch, Geschichte und Französisch lernen.
In my opinion school life is stressful but I intend to find a good job in the future, so I will continue with my studies next year. I am going to study English, history and French.

Möchtest du auf die Universität gehen? Warum (nicht)?
Would you like to go to university? Why (not)?

Als ich jünger war, wollte ich auf die Uni gehen, um Jura zu studieren, aber jetzt habe ich mich anders entschieden. Die Studiengebühren sind zu teuer.
When I was younger, I wanted to go to university to study law, but now I have changed my mind. The fees are too expensive.

Ist es wichtig für junge Leute, auf die Universität zu gehen?
Is it important for young people to go to university?

Ja, natürlich. Es kann nützlich sein, ein Diplom zu haben, aber Arbeitgeber wollen auch Arbeiter, die nicht nur gute Qualifikationen, sondern auch Berufserfahrung haben.
Yes, of course. It can be useful to have a degree, but employers want employees who don't just have good qualifications but also work experience.

Ist ein Auslandsjahr eine gute Idee?
Is a gap year a good idea?

Ein Auslandsjahr ist eine tolle Möglichkeit, um die Welt zu sehen. Man könnte eine neue Fremdsprache lernen, reisen oder im Ausland arbeiten.
A gap year is an amazing opportunity to see the world. You could learn a new language, travel or work abroad.

> Ist das Studentenleben zu teuer? Warum (nicht)?
> Is student life too expensive? Why (not)?

> Meine Schwester hat ihr Studium erfolgreich abgeschlossen, aber sie hat jetzt hohe Schulden und ist im Moment arbeitslos. Ich würde lieber eine Lehre machen – vielleicht als Mechaniker(in).
> My sister successfully completed her degree, but she now has a lot of debt and is currently unemployed. I would prefer to do an apprenticeship – maybe as a mechanic.

In this unit you may need to understand and use persuasive language and you will also want to ask questions.
Here are a few useful phrases in German:

Expressing hope
- Ich hoffe, dass … – I hope that …

Seeking/giving information
- Könnten Sie mir sagen …? – Could you tell me …?
- Gibt es …? – Is there …?
- Um wieviel Uhr …? – At what time …?

Expressing intention
- Ich werde + **infinitive** (at end of sentence) – I am going to
- Ich habe vor – I intend to

Expressing interest
- Ich interessiere mich für – I am interested in
- Ich habe eine Leidenschaft für – I am passionate about

EXAM TASK

Translate the following sentences into English:
1. Ich musste einen Bewerbungsbrief schreiben. Er war zu lang.
2. Mein Onkel hatte letzte Woche ein Bewerbungsgespräch und er war sehr nervös.
3. Meine Lehrer waren wirklich hilfsbereit.
4. Ich möchte eine neue Sprache lernen. Leider habe ich nicht genug Zeit.
5. Mein Lebenslauf ist ziemlich interessant.

Watch out for intensifiers – e.g. **zu** (too), **wirklich** (really), **sehr** (very), **ziemlich** (quite) – and make sure you translate them.

POST-16 STUDY

Ich werde an einer anderen Schule weiterlernen.	I will study at another school.
Für die meisten jungen Leute sind Studiengebühren zu teuer.	For most young people, tuition fees are too expensive.
Ich würde lieber die Schule verlassen und meine eigene Firma gründen.	I would prefer to leave school and set up my own business.
Meine Eltern glauben, dass Qualifikationen am wichtigsten sind.	My parents believe that qualifications are the most important thing.
Vielleicht werde ich im Ausland studieren.	Perhaps I will study abroad.
Ich werde die Schule verlassen und arbeiten, um Geld zu verdienen.	I'm going to leave school and work to earn some money.
Ich möchte ein Auslandsjahr machen.	I would like to take a gap year.
Ich möchte weiterstudieren, aber ich weiß nicht, welche Universität am besten für mich ist.	I would like to continue my studies but I don't know which university is best for me.
Arbeitgeber haben keine Zeit, einen langen Lebenslauf zu lesen.	Employers don't have time to read a long CV.
Grammatikfehler machen einen schlechten Eindruck.	Grammatical errors create a bad impression.
Man muss die Wahrheit sagen.	You have to tell the truth.
Ich habe die Anzeige auf der Webseite gelesen.	I read the advert on the website.
Man braucht kein Diplom für viele Berufe.	You don't need a degree for many jobs.
Ich will meine Prüfungen bestehen und erfolgreich sein.	I want to do my exams and be successful.
Freiwilligenarbeit kann bei der Berufsentscheidung helfen.	Voluntary work can help you make a career decision.
Ich hoffe, dass ich meine Prüfungen bestehen werde.	I hope that I will pass my exams.
Wenn ich meine Prüfungen nicht bestehe, werde ich eine Lehre machen.	If I don't pass my exams, I will do an apprenticeship.

In the speaking exam, don't worry if you don't understand the question at first. You won't lose marks if you ask your teacher to repeat what they said.

Here are some useful phrases in German:

- Ich habe ... nicht verstanden – I didn't understand …
- Ich verstehe ... nicht – I don't understand …
- Kannst du das bitte wiederholen? – Can you please repeat that? (informal)
- Können Sie das bitte wiederholen? – Could you please repeat that? (formal/polite)
- Was bedeutet das? – What does that mean?
- Wie bitte?/Bitte? – Sorry/pardon?
- Es tut mir leid – I'm sorry
- Was hast du gesagt? – What did you say? (informal)
- Was haben Sie gesagt? – What did you say? (formal/polite)

EXAM TASK

Here are some examples of conversation questions:

- **Möchtest du nächstes Jahr weiterstudieren? Warum (nicht)?** Do you want to continue your studies next year? Why (not)?
- **Was möchtest du als Beruf machen?** What do you want to do as a job?
- **Möchtest du zur Universität gehen? Warum (nicht)?** Do you want to go to university? Why (not)?
- **Warum hast du deine Fächer gewählt?** Why did you choose your subjects?
- **Die Schule ist eine gute Vorbereitung für die Zukunft. Was sagst du dazu?** School is a good preparation for the future. What do you think?
- **Was sind deine Stärken und Schwächen?** What are your strengths and weaknesses?

CAREER PLANS

Was möchtest du in der Zukunft machen?
What would you like to do in the future?

> Wenn ich meine Prüfungen bestehe, habe ich vor, auf die Universität zu gehen. Nach meinem Studium möchte ich einen interessanten Beruf finden und viel Geld verdienen!
> If I pass my exams, I intend to go to university. After my studies, I would like to find an interesting job and earn lots of money!

Ist es schwer, einen guten Beruf zu finden? Warum (nicht)?
Is it hard to find a good job? Why (not)?

> Es ist sehr schwer für junge Leute, einen Job zu finden. Zur Zeit gibt es eine hohe Arbeitslosigkeit in meiner Gegend. Ich habe viele Freunde, die arbeitslos sind.
> It's very difficult for young people to find a job. At the moment, there is high unemployment in my area. I have lots of friends who are unemployed.

Möchtest du im Ausland arbeiten? Warum (nicht)?
Would you like to work abroad? Why (not)?

> Meiner Meinung nach ist es eine gute Idee, im Ausland zu arbeiten, weil man neue Fähigkeiten lernen kann. Persönlich möchte ich in Australien arbeiten, weil es dort viele Möglichkeiten gibt.
> In my opinion, working abroad is a good idea because you can learn new skills. Personally, I would like to work in Australia because there are lots of opportunities there.

Was wirst du in zehn Jahren machen?
What do you want to do in ten years?

> Ich hoffe, dass ich in zehn Jahren glücklich und reich sein werde. Ich werde in einem großen Haus mit einem riesigen Schwimmbad wohnen. Ich möchte heiraten und Kinder haben.
> I hope that in ten years I will be happy and rich. I will live in a big house with a huge swimming pool. I would like to get married and have children.

Was wolltest du machen, als du jünger warst?
What did you want to do when you were younger?

Als ich jünger war, wollte ich Sänger(in) sein, weil ich berühmt sein wollte. Jetzt ist es mein Traum, in einem Krankenhaus zu arbeiten. Etwas ganz anderes!
When I was younger I wanted to be a singer because I wanted to be famous. Now it's my dream to work in a hospital. Something quite different!

Here are some useful phrases for discussing your future:

in der Zukunft – in the future
erstens – firstly
zweitens – secondly
dann – then
danach – afterwards/after that
nach dem Studium – after my studies
nach meinen Prüfungen – after my exams
nächstes Jahr – next year
mit 18 – at the age of 18

Future plans

Write a paragraph about your future plans. Use all of the time phrases on the left to sequence your paragraph and use all of the structures on the right at least once each. You can use them in any order.

- in der Zukunft
- erstens
- danach
- nach den Prüfungen
- nächstes Jahr
- mit 30

Ich werde + infinitive
Ich möchte + infinitive
Ich will + infinitive
Ich würde + infinitive

EXAM TASK

Answer the questions.

Mari: Ich möchte heiraten[1] und Kinder haben.

Lena: Nach dem Abitur möchte ich Informatik studieren.

Kim: Es gibt nicht genug[2] Arbeitsplätze in meinem Dorf.

Thomas: Ich möchte in einem Altersheim arbeiten. Ich werde kein Geld dafür bekommen, aber das ist mir egal.

Christian: Ich möchte meine Sprachkenntnisse verbessern[3].

Gwen: Ich würde viele Länder besuchen, wenn ich genug Geld hätte.

1 to marry
2 enough
3 to improve

Who …?

1. is worried about unemployment?
2. is interested in computers?
3. would like to travel?
4. wants to do voluntary work?
5. wants children?
6. wants to improve their language skills?

CAREER PLANS

USEFUL PHRASES

Wenn ich mit dem Studium fertig bin, werde ich einen guten Beruf mit einem guten Gehalt suchen.	When I finish my studies, I will look for a good job with a high salary.
Ich würde lieber meine eigene Firma haben.	I would prefer to have my own company.
Ich werde Geld sparen, um ein Haus zu kaufen.	I am going to save to buy a house.
Ich möchte in meiner Heimatstadt arbeiten, weil meine Freunde hier sind.	I would like to work in my home town because my friends are here.
Ich muss zugeben, dass ich keine Ahnung habe, was ich beruflich machen möchte.	I must admit I don't have any idea what I would like to do as a job.
Ich habe mich noch nicht entschieden, was ich später machen werde.	I haven't yet decided what I will do later.
Ich will nicht arbeitslos sein.	I don't want to be unemployed.
Mein innigster Wunsch war, Lehrer(in) zu werden.	My dearest wish was to become a teacher.
Ich möchte keinen eintönigen Beruf haben.	I don't want to have a monotonous job.
Ich will eine interessante Karriere machen.	I want to pursue an exciting career.
Nach dem Studium möchte ich in Australien wohnen.	After my studies, I would like to live in Australia.
Ich möchte im Ausland arbeiten, um meine Sprachkenntnisse zu verbessern.	I'd like to work abroad to improve my language skills.
Eines Tages möchte ich um die Welt reisen.	One day I would like to travel the world.
Als ich zehn Jahre alt war, wollte ich Astronaut(in) werden.	When I was ten, I wanted to be an astronaut.
Meiner Meinung nach lohnt es sich.	In my opinion, it's worth it.

You may need to read or write a letter of application in this unit. Here are some useful phrases in German:

- Ich habe Ihre Anzeige in der Zeitung gelesen – I read your advert in the newspaper
- Ich habe Erfahrung in … – I have experience in …
- Ich möchte hier arbeiten, weil … – I would like to work here because …
- Ich interessiere mich für diese Stelle – I am interested in this job
- Im Anhang finden Sie meinen Lebenslauf – You will find attached my CV

If you can use these phrases in your exam they will show off your ability to use different tenses.

EXAM TASK

Translate the following paragraph into German:

I'm not going to go to sixth form because it's boring. I'm going to leave school as soon as possible. Work experience is more important than qualifications. It's easy to find a good job in my town. I would like to work in an office to improve my computer skills.

GRAMMAR

GRAMMAR TERMS

It's important to understand what these terms mean as they will be used regularly throughout your GCSE course.

Adjectives: Adjectives describe nouns. They answer the questions: which, what kind of, how many – e.g. big.

Adverbs: Adverbs describe verbs (and sometimes adjectives and other adverbs). They answer the questions: how, when, where – e.g. regularly.

Articles: These are the words **the** (definite article) and **a/an** (indefinite article).

Comparative: This is a form of an adjective, which is used to compare two things – e.g. better.

Connective/conjunction: This is a word or phrase that connects two other words or parts of a sentence – e.g. because.

Demonstratives: These are words that demonstrate (point out) – e.g. this, that, these, those.

Gender: Unlike in English, nouns in German have different genders. They are masculine, feminine or neuter.

Imperative: The form of verb used when giving instructions or commands.

Infinitive: This is the form of verb you find in the dictionary. In English it always has the word **to** in front of it – e.g. to study – and in German it usually ends in **-en** or **-n**.

Irregular verb: A verb that does not follow regular patterns and has a different form when conjugated or used in different tenses. These usually need to be learnt by heart.

Noun: A person, place, thing or idea.

Object: The person or thing in a sentence that has the action happen to it.

Plural: More than one of an item.

Possessives: These are words that imply ownership – e.g. my house.

Prepositions: These are words that help to describe something's location or give other information – e.g. in, on.

Pronouns: These are words that take the place of nouns in a sentence to avoid repetition.

Reflexive verbs: Reflexive verbs describe actions the subject of the sentence does to themselves – e.g. sich waschen (to wash), sich anziehen (to get dressed).

Singular: Refers to only one of an item – as opposed to plural for more than one.

Subject: The person or thing in a sentence that's doing the action.

Superlative: The superlative is *the most* of something – e.g. best, worst, biggest.

Synonyms: Words which share the same meaning are synonyms.

Tense: This is a change in the verb to describe actions happening in the past, present, future or conditional.

Verbs: These are the action words which are doing something in a sentence.

Don't panic when you see the following grammar list! This is a list of **every** grammar point that might come up at GCSE. You won't need to use all of these grammar points yourself, but it will help if you are able to recognise different linguistic features. This reference section means that you can look up any grammar terms that are confusing you. There are also some grammar exercises throughout so that you can practise your knowledge. The verb tables at the back of this section will be useful when you are revising for your speaking and writing exams.

NOUNS AND CASES

GENDER OF NOUNS

Nouns are words that name a person, place or thing. In German all nouns are either masculine, feminine or neuter. All nouns in German start with a capital letter.

DEFINITE AND INDEFINITE ARTICLE

The definite and indefinite article (the words for **the** and **a/an**) depend on the gender of the noun:

- der/ein Computer (masculine)
- die/eine App (feminine)
- das/ein Handy (neuter)

POSSESSIVE AND DEMONSTRATIVE ADJECTIVES

Possessive adjectives show ownership – e.g. my, his. To use the correct possessive adjective you need to know:

- Which one is needed – e.g. mein, dein, sein.
- What gender the noun is – e.g. meine Schwester ist ..., mein Bruder ist ...
- The case your noun is going to be in.

Possessive adjectives include:

> mein – my
> dein – your (singular, informal)
> sein – his/its
> ihr – her
> unser – our
> euer – your (plural)
> Ihr – your (formal)

- Possessive adjectives follow the same pattern as ein/kein.
- Demonstrative adjectives like dieser (this) and jeder (every/each) follow this pattern:

	Masculine	Feminine	Neuter	Plural
Nominative	dieser	diese	dieses	diese
Accusative	diesen	diese	dieses	diese
Genitive	dieses	dieser	dieses	dieser
Dative	diesem	dieser	diesem	diesen

PLURAL OF NOUNS

The plural form of the definite article (der/die/das) is always die.

In German there are several different forms of plural nouns. There are some patterns but it's best to also learn the gender and the plural form when you are learning new nouns.

- For most feminine words, add -n or -en – e.g. Drogen.
- For most masculine words, add -e – e.g. Filme.
- For many 'foreign' words, add -s – e.g. Restaurants.
- For the dative plural, all nouns need an extra -n or -en – e.g. den Häusern.

WEAK NOUNS

These are nouns which add -n to every case apart from the nominative singular. Some common weak nouns include Junge, Herr, Mensch, Name.

CASES

There are four cases in German:

1. **Nominative** is used for the subject of the verb – e.g. **Der Computer** ist modern.
2. **Accusative** is used for the direct object of the verb and after certain prepositions – e.g. Ich kaufe **einen Computer**.
3. **Genitive** is used to show position and after certain prepositions – e.g. Der Computer **meines Freundes**.
4. **Dative** is used for the indirect object of the verb, after certain prepositions and certain verbs – e.g. Ich habe **ihm** Geld gegeben.

The following tables will help you.

Definite article (der/die/das – the)

	Masculine	Feminine	Neuter	Plural
Nominative	der	die	das	die
Accusative	den	die	das	die
Genitive	des	der	des	der
Dative	dem	der	dem	den

Indefinite article (ein/eine/ein – a/an)

	Masculine	Feminine	Neuter	Plural
Nominative	ein	eine	ein	-
Accusative	einen	eine	ein	-
Genitive	eines	einer	eines	-
Dative	einem	einer	einem	-

Negatives (the word kein (no) follows the same pattern as the indefinite article but has a plural)

	Masculine	Feminine	Neuter	Plural
Nominative	kein	keine	kein	keine
Accusative	keinen	keine	kein	keine
Genitive	keines	keiner	keines	keiner
Dative	keinem	keiner	keinem	keinen

PREPOSITIONS

Prepositions give information about the position of a noun or pronoun. They change the case of the noun or pronoun. Prepositions often have more than one meaning – e.g.:

- mit dem Taxi – by taxi
- mit meinem Bruder – with my brother

Some prepositions are always followed by the accusative case – e.g. für, um, durch, bis, ohne, wider, gegen, entlang.

Some prepositions are always followed by the dative case – e.g. bei, aus, nach, gegenüber, seit, von, außer, mit, zu.

Some prepositions are followed by the accusative or dative case depending on the meaning – e.g. an, auf, hinter, vor, in, unter, über neben, zwischen.

- Ich gehe in die Stadt. I am going to town. (accusative – movement towards)
- Ich bin in der Stadt. I am in town. (dative – indicating position)

Some prepositions are always followed by the genitive case – e.g. statt, trotz, während, wegen.

GRAMMAR

Choose the correct preposition from the list below to complete the sentence.

1. Es gibt oft Staus ___ der Stadtmitte.
2. Fahren Sie ____ der U-Bahn.
3. Es ist ____ dem Kino.
4. Sie interessiert sich ____ Geschichte.
5. Geh ___ Fuß.
6. Ich komme ___ einer Großstadt.

zu   in   neben   mit   für   aus

PRONOUNS

Pronouns can replace a noun in a sentence to avoid repetition.

- I saw a film last week. The film was good.
- I saw a film last week. **It** was good.

Pronouns change in German depending on the case.

Nominative	Accusative	Dative
ich (I)	mich (me)	mir (me)
du (you)	dich (you)	dir (you)
er (he)	ihn (him)	ihm (him)
sie (she)	sie (her)	ihr (her)
es (it)	es (it)	ihm (it)
wir (we)	uns (us)	uns (us)
ihr (you (informal plural))	euch (you (informal plural))	euch (you (informal plural))
Sie (you (formal))	Sie (you (formal))	Ihnen (you (formal))
sie (they)	sie (them)	ihnen (them)

Although **man** literally translates as **one**, it is a far more commonly used pronoun in German. It is used where we may use **you** in English.

> **Man** bekommt eine Ermäßigung. You get a discount. (One gets a discount.)
> **Man** kann mit dem Bus fahren. You can go by bus. (One can go by bus.)

Jemand is a singular pronoun meaning somebody or someone. **Niemand** is a singular pronoun meaning nobody or no one. These pronouns usually take the ending **-en** in the accusative case and **-em** in the dative case.

VERBS

PRESENT TENSE – REGULAR

The present tense is used to describe something that's happening now – e.g. **Ich lerne Deutsch**, or something that happens regularly – e.g. **Ich gehe jeden Samstag ins Kino.**

Regular verbs follow the same pattern. Take the **-en** off the infinitive (e.g. wohnen → wohn) and add the following endings to the verb stem:

> ich wohn**e**
> du wohn**st**
> er/sie/es/man wohn**t**
> wir wohn**en**
> ihr wohn**t**
> Sie wohn**en**
> sie wohn**en**

If the stem ends in **-t** you need to add an extra **e** in the du, er/sie/es/man and ihr forms.

> arbeiten (infinitive) → arbeit (stem)
> er arbeit**et**

PRESENT TENSE – IRREGULAR

Irregular verbs have almost the same endings as regular verbs but may change the form of the stem in the du, er/sie/es/man and ihr forms. See the verb tables on pages 129–133 for details.

> fahren – du fährst, sie fährt
> nehmen – du nimmst, er nimmt
> geben – du gibst, er gibt

Replace the infinitive with the correct form of the verb.

1. Ich **tragen** modische Kleidung.
2. Ich **hören** überall Musik.
3. Ich **surfen** im Internet.
4. Wir **gehen** ins Einkaufszentrum.
5. Er **schreiben** E-Mails.
6. Ich **besuchen** Chatrooms.

PRESENT TENSE – **HABEN** AND **SEIN**

Two very important irregular verbs are **haben** and **sein** – these are often used and need to be learnt.

haben – to have

ich habe	I have
du hast	you have
er/sie/es/man hat	he/she/it/one has
wir haben	we have
ihr habt	you have (informal plural)
Sie haben	you have (formal)
sie haben	they have

sein – to be

ich bin	I am
du bist	you are
er/sie/es/man ist	he/she/it/one is
wir sind	we are
ihr seid	you are (informal plural)
Sie sind	you are (formal)
sie sind	they are

SEPARABLE AND INSEPARABLE VERBS

Some verbs in German have a separable prefix which usually goes to the end of the sentence:

- **fernsehen** – to watch TV
  Ich **sehe** jeden Abend **fern**.
- **anfangen** – to start/begin
  Die Schule **fängt** um 8 Uhr **an**.
- **ankommen** – to arrive
  Ich **komme** immer pünktlich **an**.

Some verbs look like separable verbs but the prefix doesn't go to the end of the sentence. Verbs starting with **ver-**, **be-**, **emp-**, **zer-**, **ent-** and **ge-** are inseparable.

- **bekommen** – to get/receive
  Ich **bekomme** viele Hausaufgaben. I get a lot of homework.
- **verstehen** – to understand
  Ich **verstehe** das nicht. I don't understand that.

- **gewinnen** – to win
  Er **gewinnt** immer. He always wins.

REFLEXIVE VERBS AND PRONOUNS

Some verbs in German are reflexive (they describe an action the subject does to themselves) and need a reflexive pronoun. Most use the **accusative** form of the reflexive pronoun:

- Ich interessiere **mich** für Musik.
- Er wäscht **sich**.
- Sie zieht **sich** an.

But a few use the **dative** form:

- Ich mache **mir** Sorgen um Heidi.
- Ich putze **mir** die Zähne.

Reflexive pronouns

Subject	Accusative	Dative
ich	mich	mir
du	dich	dir
er/sie/es/man	sich	sich
wir	uns	uns
ihr	euch	euch
Sie	sich	sich
sie	sich	sich

PERFECT TENSE

The perfect tense is used to talk about things which happened in the past. It is the most common way to talk about the past in German.

To form the perfect tense you need:

- the correct form of haben or sein
- a past participle

There are regular (e.g. **gespielt, gewohnt**) and irregular (e.g. **gegangen, gesehen**) past participles:

- Ich **habe** im Park **gespielt**.
- Er **hat** in der Stadtmitte **gewohnt**.
- Ich **habe** einen Film **gesehen**.

Some verbs (see the verb tables on pages 128–133) use **sein** instead of **haben**. These are usually verbs of movement – e.g. kommen, gehen, fahren, fliegen.

- Ich **bin** ins Kino **gegangen**.
- Wir **sind** mit dem Bus **gefahren**.

Separable verbs join back together to form the past participle:

- Ich habe ferngesehen.
- Der Zug ist pünktlich angekommmen.

Inseparable verbs don't need **ge-** to form the past participle:

- Ich habe meine Tante **besucht**.
- Meine Mannschaft hat **gewonnen**.

GRAMMAR

Complete the perfect tense sentences using the correct form of haben or sein.

1. Ich _____ CDs gekauft.
2. Ich _____ ins Restaurant gegangen.
3. Er ___ einen Film gesehen.
4. Wir _____ ins Kino gegangen.
5. Ich _____ in Frankreich gewohnt.
6. Meine Schwester _____ Kleidung gekauft.

Put these present tense sentences into the perfect tense.

Example: Ich wohne in Berlin. → Ich habe in Berlin gewohnt.

1. Ich mache meinen Führerschein.
2. Ich fahre mit dem Rad.
3. Ich finde Autos sehr laut.
4. Mein Bruder geht zu Fuß in die Stadt.
5. Wir fliegen nach Spanien.

Put these present tense sentences into the perfect tense.

1. Mein Bruder sieht gern fern.
2. Meine Schwester besucht das Stadion.
3. Ich lade Fotos hoch.
4. Er lädt Musik herunter.
5. Ich benutze oft das Internet.

IMPERFECT TENSE

The imperfect tense is used more often in formal writing (books, newspapers, etc.). However, certain common verbs are more likely to be used in the imperfect tense in speech and less formal writing.

> ich war – I was
> es war – it was
> ich hatte – I had
> es hatte – it had
> es gab – there was

For regular verbs, add the following endings to the stem:

> spielen (infinitive) → spiel (stem)
> ich spielte
> du spieltest
> er/sie/es/man spielte
> wir spielten
> ihr spieltet
> Sie spielten
> sie spielten

For irregular verbs, add the following endings to the changed stem (see the verb tables on pages 128–133):

> fahren (infinitive) → fuhr (changed stem)
> ich fuhr
> du fuhrst
> er/sie/es/man fuhr
> wir fuhren
> ihr fuhrt
> Sie fuhren
> sie fuhren

When using modal verbs to talk about events in the past you usually need to use the imperfect tense. Here are the ich forms:

> ich konnte – I could
> ich durfte – I was allowed to
> ich sollte – I was supposed to
> ich musste – I had to
> ich wollte – I wanted to
> ich mochte – I liked

GRAMMAR

Complete the sentences using **hatte** or **war**.

1. Ich _____ viele Hausaufgaben.
2. Ich ____ nervös, weil ich eine Prüfung _____.
3. Er _____ nicht genug Zeit.
4. Ich _____ keine Lust, Grammatik zu lernen.
5. Es _____ sehr kompliziert.
6. Ich ____ müde.

Choose the correct word from the list below to complete each sentence.

1. Ich _____ Kopfschmerzen.
2. Es _____ gestern sonnig.
3. Ich _____ eine neue Batterie kaufen.
4. Es ____ viele Probleme.
5. Wir _____ Hunger.

hatten   gab   war   hatte   musste

PLUPERFECT TENSE

The pluperfect tense is used to describe something that has already happened, usually at an earlier point in the past.

To form it you use the imperfect form of **haben** or **sein** with a past participle:

- Ich hatte einen Tisch reserviert. I had reserved a table.
- Ich hatte schon gegessen. I had already eaten.
- Ich war zur Party gegangen. I had gone to the party.

FUTURE TENSE

The future tense is formed in the same way with irregular verbs and regular verbs. The future tense is easily formed by using the correct form of **werden** plus an infinitive at the end of the sentence:

ich werde	I will
du wirst	you will
er/sie/es/man wird	he/she/it/one will
wir werden	we will
ihr werdet	you will (informal plural)
Sie werden	you will (formal)
sie werden	they will

- Ich **werde** am Samstag neue Kleidung **kaufen**.
- Ich **werde** Jeans und ein T-shirt **tragen**.

In German the present tense can also be used to talk about events in the future. However, it needs to be clear that you are talking about the future – usually a time phrase will indicate this.

- Ich gehe **nächste Woche** auf die Party.
- Wir gehen **nächsten Samstag** ins Kino.

GRAMMAR

Rearrange the words to form future tense sentences.

1. Computerspiele ich werde spielen.
2. Handy mein ein neues Bruder kaufen wird.
3. gehen werden wir ins Kino.
4. sie einen wird kaufen 3D-Drucker.
5. Autos der Zukunft brauchen werden keinen Fahrer.

CONDITIONAL TENSE

The conditional tense is used to say what you would do, if possible under given conditions – e.g. I would build more houses (to improve my town). The conditional tense is formed in the same way with irregular verbs and regular verbs – e.g. Ich **würde** mehr Häuser **bauen** (, um meine Stadt zu verbessern).

Use the correct form of würden plus an infinitive at the end of the sentence:

> ich würde gehen
> du würdest gehen
> er/sie/es/man würde gehen
> wir würden gehen
> ihr würdet gehen
> Sie würden gehen
> sie würden gehen

When using haben and sein in the conditional to say what you would do or have, the verbs take the following forms:

haben	sein
ich hätte	ich wäre
du hättest	du wärest
er/sie/es/man hätte	er/sie/es/man wäre
wir hätten	wir wären
ihr hättet	ihr wäret
Sie hätten	Sie wären
sie hätten	sie wären

- Wenn ich reich wäre, würde ich ein modernes Haus kaufen. If I were rich, I would buy a modern house.
- Wenn ich mehr Geld hätte, würde ich umziehen. If I had more money, I'd move.

Ich möchte is a useful phrase meaning 'I would like to …' It is often used with an infinitive at the end of the sentence.

> Ich möchte mit 21 heiraten.
> Ich möchte in der Zukunft Kinder haben.

GRAMMAR

Put these present tense sentences into the conditional tense.

1. Ich wasche Autos.
2. Er spendet Geld.
3. Die Organisation verdient mehr Geld.
4. Es ist besser.
5. Ich habe nicht genug Zeit.

IMPERATIVES (COMMANDS)

The imperative is used to give commands or instructions.

With the Sie form, you just use the present tense and switch the verb and pronoun:

- **Sie wählen** eine Sprache. → **Wählen Sie** eine Sprache! Choose a language!
- **Gehen Sie** geradeaus! Go straight on!
- **Vergessen Sie** nicht! Don't forget!

Separable verbs

- **Rufen Sie** uns **an**. Give us a call.

With the du form, you just use the present tense verb and take the -st off. You might also see this with an -e added in written German:

- **Buch(e)** sofort. Book straight away.
- **Besuch(e)** die Altstadt. Visit the old city.

Remember that some verbs are irregular in the du form:

- **Nimm** den Bus. Take the bus.
- **Lies** die Werbung. Read the advert.

MODAL VERBS

The modal verbs are:

> dürfen – to be allowed to
> können – to be able to
> müssen – to have to (must)
> wollen – to want to
> sollen – to be supposed to
> mögen – to like to

They are usually used with an infinitive at the end of the sentence:

- Man **darf** mit 18 **heiraten**.
- Mein Bruder **kann** Auto **fahren**.
- Ich **muss** meine Tante **besuchen**.

	dürfen	können	müssen	wollen	sollen	mögen
ich	darf	kann	muss	will	soll	mag
du	darfst	kannst	musst	willst	sollst	magst
er/sie/es/man	darf	kann	muss	will	soll	mag
wir	dürfen	können	müssen	wollen	sollen	mögen
ihr	dürft	könnt	müsst	wollt	sollt	mögt
Sie	dürfen	können	müssen	wollen	sollen	mögen
sie	dürfen	können	müssen	wollen	sollen	mögen

IMPERSONAL VERBS

Some common impersonal verbs are often used in the **es** form:

> Es gibt viel zu tun. There is lots to do.
> Es geht mir gut. I am well.
> Es tut mir leid. I'm sorry.
> Es schmeckt mir. It's tasty.
> Es gefällt mir. I like it.
> Es tut weh. It hurts.
> Es regnet. It's raining.
> Es schneit. It's snowing.

Translate the sentences into English.

1. Es gibt ein Kino in der Stadtmitte.
2. Es gab nicht viel für junge Leute.
3. Es tut mir leid.
4. Es gefällt mir gut.
5. Es hat mir gut geschmeckt.

INFINITIVE CONSTRUCTIONS

Um … zu … is a really useful structure in German. It means 'in order to' (although we often miss that out in English).

• Ich benutze das Internet, **um** Computerspiele **zu** kaufen. I use the internet (in order) to buy computer games.

The verb in the um … zu … clause is always an infinitive and goes at the end of the sentence.
Ohne zu … is also used with an infinitive. It means 'without doing something'.

• Er hat mein Handy genommen, **ohne zu** fragen. He took my mobile phone without asking.

Zu is sometimes needed before the infinitive in a sentence. It means 'to'.

• Ich hoffe, ein Auto **zu** gewinnen. I hope to win a car.
• Ich verspreche, alles **zu** geben. I promise to give everything.

Verbs which need this include:

> hoffen – to hope
> versprechen – to promise
> Lust haben – to fancy
> beginnen – to begin

Complete the sentences using the correct verb from the list.

1. Ich werde nächstes Jahr Geschichte _____.
2. Ich habe letztes Jahr Mathe _____.
3. Ich _____ gern Sport.
4. Ich _____ gestern nicht genug Zeit.
5. Es ___ langweilig.
6. Ich _____ eine neue Sprache lernen, wenn ich mehr Zeit _____.

würde   hatte   lernen   mache   gelernt   war   hätte

ADJECTIVES AND ADVERBS

ADJECTIVES

Adjectives give more information about a noun.

If an adjective is used after the noun it does not change.

- Mein Lehrer ist **interessant**.
- Meine Lehrerin ist **interessant**.

However, adjective endings change when used before a noun.

Adjective endings with the definite article

	Masculine	Feminine	Neuter	Plural
Nominative	der alt**e** Mann	die alt**e** Frau	das alt**e** Haus	die alt**en** Leute
Accusative	den alt**en** Mann	die alt**e** Frau	das alt**e** Haus	die alt**en** Leute
Genitive	des alt**en** Mannes	der alt**en** Frau	des alt**en** Hauses	der alt**en** Leute
Dative	dem alt**en** Mann	der alt**en** Frau	dem alt**en** Haus	den alt**en** Leuten

Adjective endings with the indefinite article (and kein)

	Masculine	Feminine	Neuter	Plural
Nominative	ein alt**er** Mann	eine alt**e** Frau	ein alt**es** Haus	keine alt**en** Leute
Accusative	einen alt**en** Mann	eine alt**e** Frau	ein alt**es** Haus	keine alt**en** Leute
Genitive	eines alt**en** Mannes	einer alt**en** Frau	eines alt**en** Hauses	keiner alt**en** Leute
Dative	einem alt**en** Mann	einer alt**en** Frau	einem alt**en** Haus	keinen alt**en** Leuten

Adjective endings with no article

	Masculine	Feminine	Neuter	Plural
Nominative	schwarz**er** Kaffee	klein**e** Tasse	gut**es** Essen	kalt**e** Snacks
Accusative	schwarz**en** Kaffee	klein**e** Tasse	gut**es** Essen	kalt**e** Snacks
Genitive	schwarz**en** Kaffees	klein**er** Tasse	gut**en** Essens	kalt**en** Snacks
Dative	schwarz**em** Kaffee	klein**er** Tasse	gut**em** Essen	kalt**en** Snacks

Add the correct ending to the adjective.

1. Ich trinke gern (**warm**) Getränke.
2. Es gibt ein (**türkisch**) Restaurant.
3. Ich werde (**schwarz**) Jeans tragen.
4. Wir verkaufen (**preiswert**) Snacks.
5. Buchen Sie eine (**unvergesslich**) Party!
6. Mein (**älter**) Bruder ist Vegetarier.

Adjectives can be turned into nouns by:

- Adding -e to the end of the adjective.
- Making the first letter a capital.
- Putting der, die or das in front.

  > deutsch → **der Deutsche** – the German (male), **die Deutsche** – the German (female)
  > richtig → **das Richtige** (the right thing)

- When used after certain words like etwas, nichts, wenig and viel, adjectives need a capital letter and **-es** adding to the end.

  > **nichts** Interessant**es**
  > **etwas** Gut**es**

ADVERBS

Adverbs give more information about a verb – they can describe when, how (often) or where something happened. They can be just one word – e.g. langsam, gesund.

- Der Bus fährt **langsam**.
- Wir essen **gesund**.

Adverbs of time and place include manchmal, immer, oft, hier and dort.
  Common adverbial phrases include ab und zu, letzte Woche, nächstes Wochenende and um 7 Uhr.
  Gern, lieber and am liebsten are useful ways to talk about what you like/prefer to do. They go after the verb.

- Ich fahre **gern** mit dem Rad. I like going by bike.
- Ich fahre **lieber** mit dem Auto. I prefer going by car.
- Ich fahre **am liebsten** mit dem Taxi. I like going by taxi most of all.

When used in questions they go after the subject.

- Fährst du **gern** mit dem Bus? Do you like travelling by bus?

COMPARATIVES AND SUPERLATIVES

When comparing things, with most adjectives you simply add **-er** to form the comparative:

- klein → klein**er** – smaller
- modern → modern**er** – more modern

For some (short) adjectives, you also need to add an umlaut:

- alt → **ält**er – older
- groß → **größ**er – larger

Use the word **als** to compare things:

> Das Kino ist moderner **als** das Sportzentrum.

To form the superlative you can use **am** and add **-sten** to the adjective:

- **am kleinsten** – the smallest
- **am modernsten** – the most modern
- Das Kino in der Stadt ist **am modernsten.**

However, there are also some irregular forms:

- gut, besser, am besten – good, better, the best
- viel, mehr, am meisten – a lot, more, the most

INTENSIFIERS

These words add emphasis to the adjective or adverb they are with – e.g. **sehr teuer** (very expensive), **gar nicht intelligent** (not at all intelligent).

> sehr – very
> zu – too
> viel – much
> ganz/ziemlich – quite
> ein wenig – a little
> ein bisschen – a bit
> einfach – simply
> gar nicht/überhaupt nicht – not at all

WORD ORDER

VERB AS THE SECOND IDEA

In a main clause the verb is always the second idea (but not always the second word):

- Ich **gehe** jede Woche ins Kino.
- Jede Woche **gehe** ich ins Kino.

QUESTION WORDS AND VERB INVERSION

You can ask questions in two different ways:

1. With a question word:

   wann – when
   was – was
   wo – where
   warum – why
   wie – how
   wer – who
   welcher – which

   Was lernst du in der Schule? What do you learn at school?
   Wie stressig ist die Schule? How stressful is school?

2. Or by verb inversion – switching the verb and subject:

   Lernst du gern Informatik? Do you enjoy learning IT?
   Ist Schule stressig? Is school stressful?

Note that the word for **who** can be **wer, wen** or **wem** depending on the case.

- Wer is the nominative form – e.g. **Wer** ist das?
- Wen is the accusative form – e.g. **Wen** hast du gesehen?
- Wem is the dative form – e.g. Mit **wem** bist du hier?

TIME – MANNER – PLACE

The usual order for a sentence in German when you are giving several details is as follows:

1. Time (when)
2. Manner (how)
3. Place (where)

Ich gehe (1) **jeden Tag** (2) **zu Fuß** (3) **in die Schule**.

CONJUNCTIONS – COORDINATING AND SUBORDINATING

Coordinating conjunctions don't change the word order. Some common ones are:

> und – and
> aber – but
> denn – because
> oder – or

Ich wohne in der Stadt **und** ich habe mein eigenes Auto.

Subordinating conjunctions act as verb scarers – they send the verb to the end of the sentence. Here are some common ones:

> bevor – before
> da/weil – because
> obwohl – although
> wenn – when/if
> damit – so that
> als – when (past tense)
> dass – that
> ob – if/whether
> während – whilst

Ich fahre mit dem Bus, **obwohl** er langsam **ist**.

RELATIVE CLAUSES

Relative pronouns are used to refer back to a noun from a previous clause in the sentence. In English the words **who**, **which** or **what** are usually used.

Relative pronouns send the verb to the end of the sentence. The pronoun you need to use depends on the gender of the noun you are referring back to.

> **der** – Der Tisch, **der** in der Ecke ist, ist viel zu klein.
> **die** – Die Bäckerei, **die** in der Stadt ist, ist toll!
> **das** – Mein Lieblingsrestaurant, **das** Nandos heißt, ist in der Stadtmitte.

Words like **wo** and **was** can be used to make a relative clause:

- Es gibt ein Restaurant, **wo** man Fast Food essen kann. There's a restaurant, where you can eat fast food.
- Ich weiß nicht, **was** ich machen soll. I don't know what I ought to do.

Again, the verb in the relative clause goes to the end of the sentence.

NEGATIVES

Nicht means **not** and is usually used to negate a verb:

- Ich gehe am Samstag **nicht** in die Schule.
- Er ist **nicht** groß.

Kein means **no/not a/not any** and is usually used to negate a noun:

- Ich habe **kein** Auto.
- Es gibt **keine** Bushaltestelle in meinem Dorf.

Nichts means **nothing/not anything**:

- Es gibt **nichts** zu tun.

SEIT

Seit is used with the present tense to say how long you have been doing something for:

- Ich wohne **seit** zehn Jahren in München. I have lived in Munich for ten years (and still do!).

Seit is used with the imperfect tense to say what had happened at a previous time:

- Ich wohnte **seit** einem Jahr in Dresden. I had lived for a year in Dresden.

DU, IHR AND SIE

There are three ways of saying **you** in German:

- Du is the informal version if you are talking to one person.
- Ihr is the informal version if you are talking to two or more people.
- Sie is the formal version.

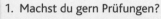

Put these questions into the Sie form.

1. Machst du gern Prüfungen?
2. Arbeitest du gern mit Kindern?
3. Wo möchtest du studieren?
4. Bekommst du Taschengeld?
5. Bist du kreativ?
6. Hast du genug Geld?

VERB TABLES

REGULAR VERBS

Regular verbs all follow the same pattern. See pages 113–121 for more details.

Infinitive		Present	Imperfect	Perfect	Future	Conditional
spielen – to play	ich	spiel**e**	spiel**te**	habe gespielt	werde spielen	würde spielen
	du	spiel**st**	spiel**test**	hast gespielt	wirst spielen	würdest spielen
	er/sie/es/man	spiel**t**	spiel**te**	hat gespielt	wird spielen	würde spielen
	wir	spiel**en**	spiel**ten**	haben gespielt	werden spielen	würden spielen
	ihr	spiel**t**	spiel**tet**	habt gespielt	werdet spielen	würdet spielen
	Sie	spiel**en**	spiel**ten**	haben gespielt	werden spielen	würden spielen
	sie	spiel**en**	spiel**ten**	haben gespielt	werden spielen	würden spielen

Common regular verbs

arbeiten – to work
bauen – to build
buchen – to book/reserve
danken – to thank
folgen – to follow
frühstücken – to breakfast
holen – to fetch
hören – to hear
kaufen – to buy
kochen – to cook
lachen – to laugh
leben – to live
lernen – to learn
lieben – to love
loben – to praise
machen – to make/do

malen – to paint
nutzen – to use
putzen – to clean
regnen – to rain
reisen – to travel
sagen – to say
schicken – to send
spielen – to play
surfen – to surf
tanzen – to dance
telefonieren – to phone
träumen – to dream
wählen – to choose/vote
wandern – to hike/wander
warten – to wait
wohnen – to live

IRREGULAR VERB TABLES

Infinitive		Present	Imperfect	Perfect	Future	Conditional
		Some verbs change in the du and er/sie/es/man forms.	Irregular verbs change the stem and add the following endings.	Irregular past participles. Remember some verbs use haben and some use sein (these are indicated by an asterisk*).	The future tense is formed in the same way with regular and irregular verbs.	The conditional tense is formed in the same way with regular and irregular verbs.
helfen – to help	ich	helfe	half	habe geholfen	werde helfen	würde helfen
	du	hilf**st**	half**st**	hast geholfen	wirst helfen	würdest helfen
	er/sie/es/man	hilft	half	hat geholfen	wird helfen	würde helfen
	wir	helf**en**	half**en**	haben geholfen	werden helfen	würden helfen
	ihr	helft	half**t**	habt geholfen	werdet helfen	würdet helfen
	Sie	helf**en**	half**en**	haben geholfen	werden helfen	würden helfen
	sie	helf**en**	half**en**	haben geholfen	werden helfen	würden helfen
gehen* – to go	ich	gehe	ging	bin gegangen	werde gehen	würde gehen
	du	gehst	gingst	bist gegangen	wirst gehen	würdest gehen
	er/sie/es/man	geht	ging	ist gegangen	wird gehen	würde gehen
	wir	gehen	gingen	sind gegangen	werden gehen	würden gehen
	ihr	geht	gingt	seid gegangen	werdet gehen	würdet gehen
	Sie	gehen	gingen	sind gegangen	werden gehen	würden gehen
	sie	gehen	gingen	sind gegangen	werden gehen	würden gehen

Infinitive	Present	Imperfect (stem)	Perfect
beginnen – to begin	-	begann	hat begonnen
bieten – to offer	-	bot	hat geboten
bitten – to ask	-	bat	hat gebeten
bleiben* – to stay	-	blieb	ist geblieben*
brechen* – to break	-	brach	hat/ist gebrochen*
bringen – to bring	-	brachte	hat gebracht
denken – to think	-	dachte	hat gedacht
empfehlen – to recommend	empfiehlst empfiehlt	empfahl	hat empfohlen
essen – to eat	isst isst	aß	hat gegessen
fahren* – to go/drive	fährst fährt	fuhr	ist gefahren*
fallen* – to fall	fällst fällt	fiel	ist gefallen*
fangen – to catch	fängst fängt	fing	hat gefangen
finden – to find	-	fand	hat gefunden
fliegen* – to fly	-	flog	ist geflogen*
fliehen* – to flee	-	floh	ist geflohen*
geben – to give	gibst gibt	gab	hat gegeben
gehen* – to go	-	ging	ist gegangen*
gelingen* – to succeed	-	gelang	ist gelungen*
gelten – to count/be worth	giltst gilt	galt	hat gegolten
genießen – to enjoy	-	genoss	hat genossen
geschehen* – to happen	geschiehst geschieht	geschah	ist geschehen*
gewinnen – to win	-	gewann	hat gewonnen

Infinitive	Present	Imperfect (stem)	Perfect
halten – to hold	hältst hält	hielt	hat gehalten
heißen – to be called	-	hieß	hat geheißen
helfen – to help	hilfst hilft	half	hat geholfen
kennen – to know	-	kannte	hat gekannt
kommen* – to come	-	kam	ist gekommen*
laden – to load	lädst lädt	lud	hat geladen
lassen – to let	lässt lässt	ließ	hat gelassen
laufen* – to walk/run	läufst läuft	lief	ist gelaufen*
leiden – to suffer	-	litt	hat gelitten
leihen – to lend	-	lieh	hat geliehen
lesen – to read	liest liest	las	hat gelesen
liegen – to lie	-	lag	hat gelegen
lügen – to tell a lie	-	log	hat gelogen
nehmen – to take	nimmst nimmt	nahm	hat genommen
nennen – to name	-	nannte	hat genannt
raten – to advise	rätst rät	riet	hat geraten
reiten* – to ride	-	ritt	ist geritten*
rennen* – to run	-	rannte	ist gerannt*
rufen – to call	-	rief	hat gerufen
schaffen – to create	-	schuf	hat geschaffen
scheiden* – to separate/divorce	-	schied	ist geschieden*
scheinen – to shine	-	schien	hat geschienen

Infinitive	Present	Imperfect (stem)	Perfect
schlafen – to sleep	schläfst schläft	schlief	hat geschlafen
schlagen – to hit/beat	schlägst schlägt	schlug	hat geschlagen
schließen – to close/shut	-	schloss	hat geschlossen
schreiben – to write	-	schrieb	hat geschrieben
schwimmen* – to swim	-	schwamm	ist geschwommen*
sehen – to see	siehst sieht	sah	hat gesehen
singen – to sing	-	sang	hat gesungen
sitzen – to sit	-	saß	hat gesessen
sprechen – to speak	sprichst spricht	sprach	hat gesprochen
stehen – to stand	-	stand	hat gestanden
stehlen – to steal	stiehlst stiehlt	stahl	hat gestohlen
steigen* – to climb/rise	-	stieg	ist gestiegen*
sterben* – to die	stirbst stirbt	starb	ist gestorben*
streiten – to argue	-	stritt	hat gestritten
tragen – to carry/wear	trägst trägt	trug	hat getragen
treffen – to meet	triffst trifft	traf	hat getroffen
treiben – to do (sport)	-	trieb	hat getrieben
trinken – to drink	-	trank	hat getrunken
tun – to do	-	tat	hat getan
vergessen – to forget	vergisst vergisst	vergaß	hat vergessen
verlieren – to lose	-	verlor	hat verloren

Infinitive	Present	Imperfect (stem)	Perfect
verschwinden* – to disappear	-	verschwand	ist verschwunden*
waschen – to wash	wäschst wäscht	wusch	hat gewaschen
werden* – to become	wirst wird	wurde	ist geworden*
werfen – to throw	wirfst wirft	warf	hat geworfen
ziehen – to pull	-	zog	hat gezogen

ANSWERS

SELF AND RELATIONSHIPS
Page 21
1. My aunt is funny, kind and sporty.
2. When I was younger, I had lots of friends.
3. He gets on well with his sister.
4. How do you get on with your family?

TECHNOLOGY AND SOCIAL MEDIA
Page 25
1. two-thirds
2. b
3. Concentration problems/poor marks in school/ illness (headache and stomach ache)/fear (list any three).

HEALTH AND FITNESS
Page 31
1. Young people and alcohol.
2. The number of 18–25-year-olds who have drunk alcohol at least once.
3. The number of 12–17-year-olds who have never drunk alcohol.
4. At least once a week.

ENTERTAINMENT AND LEISURE
Page 35
1. Timo
2. Nina
3. Nina
4. Andreas
5. Timo

Page 37
1. Letzte Woche bin ich in die Stadt einkaufen gegangen.
2. Nächstes Wochenende werde ich mit meiner Familie ins Kino gehen.
3. Was ist deine Lieblingssendung?
4. Ich kann morgen nicht ausgehen, weil ich viele Hausaufgaben habe.

FOOD AND DRINK
Page 41
1. It's in the middle of modern Europe.
2. Southern and eastern countries.
3. He wants recipes to be shared/for families to cook and eat together.
4. Time.

FESTIVALS AND CELEBRATIONS
Page 45
I was at a music festival in Munich last week. It was lots of fun, because I was with my friends. We danced for hours and made friends with people from all over Germany. The music was great and I bought a T-shirt as a souvenir. Now I understand why music festivals are so popular.

LOCAL AREAS OF INTEREST
Page 51
1. A
2. A
3. B
4. B
5. B

Page 53
Ich wohne gern in meinem Dorf. Es gibt nicht viele Geschäfte. Meine Mutter findet die Gegend langweilig, weil es kein Sportzentrum gibt. Ich werde in Spanien wohnen, wenn ich älter bin.

TRAVEL AND TRANSPORT
Page 55
1. Is it possible to travel from Hamburg to Berlin for 14 euros?
2. Germany and Europe.
3. They are 75% cheaper (than by train).
4. Better for environment/easy/fun (not so boring) (list any two).
5. Use the website or send a text.

LOCAL AND REGIONAL FEATURES AND CHARACTERISTICS OF GERMANY AND GERMAN-SPEAKING COUNTRIES
Page 61
I like visiting new countries when I go on holiday. Last year I went to Switzerland with my family. My parents are interested in history, so we visited lots of museums and historical buildings. I'd like to go to Poland next year to learn more about the culture.

HOLIDAYS AND TOURISM
Page 65
1. Markus
2. Lotte
3. Katja
4. Paul
5. Florian
6. Sofia

Page 67
1. past
2. past
3. future
4. conditional
5. present
6. present

ENVIRONMENT
Page 71
- to help
- to protect
- to reduce
- to damage
- to save
- to pollute
- to recycle
- to destroy
- to cause
- to waste
- to use

Page 71
1. It rained/there was lots of rain (30–40 litres in an hour).
2. 2500 people had to leave their homes/spend the night in the youth centre.
3. More flooding is likely/the forecast for the next three days doesn't look good.
4. There were hailstones the size of golf balls.
5. It'll be windy/very cold.

SOCIAL ISSUES
Page 75
1. Not very original/very easy.
2. Buy some cakes from the supermarket or bakery.
3. Christmas and birthday presents (unwanted)/old toys.

SCHOOL/COLLEGE LIFE
Page 81
1. Quite normal/a bit fat/wears (thick/square) glasses (list any two).
2. He hopes his glasses will break.
3. Nervous.
4. To find out what class he is in.
5. Embarrassed (he turns red)/he thinks everyone is looking at him and laughing.

SCHOOL/COLLEGE STUDIES
Page 85
1. b
2. a
3. c
4. b

EMPLOYMENT
Page 91
1. Machen Sie gern Prüfungen?
2. Arbeiten Sie gern mit Kindern?
3. Wo möchten Sie studieren?
4. Bekommen Sie Taschengeld?
5. Sind Sie kreativ?
6. Haben Sie genug Geld?

Page 91
1. A work placement in a primary school.
2. It will be good for her CV/she likes working with children.
3. Difficult to find a job/high (youth) unemployment.
4. Details about the working day/what to wear.

SKILLS AND PERSONAL QUALITIES
Page 95
1. c
2. j

3. d

4. i

5. b

6. h

7. g

8. a

9. f

10. e

POST-16 STUDY

Page 99

1. I had to write an application letter. It was too long.

2. My uncle had an interview last week and he was really nervous.

3. My teachers were really helpful.

4. I would like to learn a new language. Unfortunately, I don't have enough time.

5. My CV is quite interesting.

CAREER PLANS

Page 103

1. Kim

2. Lena

3. Gwen

4. Thomas

5. Mari

6. Christian

Page 105

Ich werde nicht in die Oberstufe gehen, weil es langweilig ist. Ich werde die Schule so bald wie möglich verlassen. Berufserfahrung ist wichtiger als Qualifikationen. Es ist einfach, eine gute Stelle in meiner Stadt zu finden. Ich möchte in einem Büro arbeiten, um meine Computerkenntnisse zu verbessern.

GRAMMAR

Page 111

1. Es gibt oft Staus **in** der Stadtmitte.

2. Fahren Sie **mit** der U-Bahn.

3. Es ist **neben** dem Kino.

4. Sie interessiert sich **für** Geschichte.

5. Geh **zu** Fuß.

6. Ich komme **aus** einer Großstadt.

Page 113

1. Ich **trage** modische Kleidung.

2. Ich **höre** überall Musik.

3. Ich **surfe** im Internet.

4. Wir **gehen** ins Einkaufszentrum.

5. Er **schreibt** E-Mails.

6. Ich **besuche** Chatrooms.

Page 116

1. Ich **habe** CDs gekauft.

2. Ich **bin** ins Restaurant gegangen.

3. Er **hat** einen Film gesehen.

4. Wir **sind** ins Kino gegangen.

5. Ich **habe** in Frankreich gewohnt.

6. Meine Schwester **hat** Kleidung gekauft.

Page 116

1. Ich habe meinen Führerschein gemacht.

2. Ich bin mit dem Rad gefahren.

3. Ich habe Autos sehr laut gefunden.

4. Mein Bruder ist zu Fuß in die Stadt gegangen.

5. Wir sind nach Spanien geflogen.

Page 116

1. Mein Bruder hat gerne ferngesehen.

2. Meine Schwester hat das Stadion besucht.

3. Ich habe Fotos hochgeladen.

4. Er hat Musik heruntergeladen.

5. Ich habe oft das Internet benutzt.

Page 117

1. Ich **hatte** viele Hausaufgaben.

2. Ich **war** nervös, weil ich eine Prüfung **hatte**.

3. Er **hatte** nicht genug Zeit.

4. Ich **hatte** keine Lust, Grammatik zu lernen.

5. Es **war** sehr kompliziert.

6. Ich **war** müde.

Page 117

1. Ich **hatte** Kopfschmerzen.

2. Es **war** gestern sonnig.

3. Ich **musste** eine neue Batterie kaufen.

4. Es **gab** viele Probleme.

5. Wir **hatten** Hunger.

Page 118

1. Ich werde Computerspiele spielen.

2. Mein Bruder wird ein neues Handy kaufen.

3. Wir werden ins Kino gehen.

4. Sie wird einen 3D-Drucker kaufen.

5. Autos der Zukunft werden keinen Fahrer brauchen.

Page 119

1. Ich würde Autos waschen.
2. Er würde Geld spenden.
3. Die Organisation würde mehr Geld verdienen.
4. Es wäre besser.
5. Ich hätte nicht genug Zeit.

Page 121

1. There is a cinema in the town centre.
2. There wasn't much for young people.
3. I'm sorry.
4. I really like it.
5. I liked the taste.

Page 121

1. Ich werde nächstes Jahr Geschichte **lernen**.
2. Ich habe letztes Jahr Mathe **gelernt**.
3. Ich **mache** gern Sport.
4. Ich **hatte** gestern nicht genug Zeit.
5. Es **war** langweilig.
6. Ich **würde** eine neue Sprache lernen, wenn ich mehr Zeit **hätte**.

Page 123

1. Ich trinke gern **warme** Getränke.
2. Es gibt ein **türkisches** Restaurant.
3. Ich werde **schwarze** Jeans tragen.
4. Wir verkaufen **preiswerte** Snacks.
5. Buchen Sie eine **unvergessliche** Party!
6. Mein **älterer** Bruder ist Vegetarier.

Page 127

1. Machen Sie gern Prüfungen?
2. Arbeiten Sie gern mit Kindern?
3. Wo möchten Sie studieren?
4. Bekommen Sie Taschengeld?
5. Sind Sie kreativ?
6. Haben Sie genug Geld?